Fly in the Buttermilk

Fly in the Buttermilk

One Black Man's Odyssey
Out On The Prairie

Rev. Robert L. Polk

Combray House

Credits
Roy Lloyd, executive editor

Editors and first readers:
Kirah Dandridge
Treadwell Merrill
Elizabeth Luntz
Vivian Maragos Zimmerman

Cover and book design
Gilbert Fletcher

ISBN 978-1-958659-01-4

Dedication

The Congregational Church of
Berthold, North Dakota 1955 – 1957

The young men and women of the Minot, N.D.
YMCA, their advisors, and staff 1957-1960

Preface

IT HAS BEEN OVER HALF a century since I resigned from my post as Youth Program Secretary of the Minot, North Dakota YMCA. Time has rushed in upon me in such a way that I can hardly believe it has already been over six decades. As I examine and reflect on my life and work on the prairie, I continue to raise the question, "How did I manage it?" I was a young, single, Black, cosmopolite from the South Side of Chicago. Called to his first pastorate out of seminary, in a tiny rural, all White town, of four hundred souls in Berthold, North Dakota. As I look back, I am startled by how this saga started in the first place. And that was just the beginning. Upon leaving that church (and town after two years), I had the audacity to accept a post in the city of Minot, ND, (population about 35K) as the youth director of its YMCA. I would be given responsibility for over three hundred teenagers.

North Dakota had the smallest population of all of the forty-eight states at that time and, furthermore, the Negro population totaled only forty-seven until I became a permanent resident in 1955. The Black population then grew to forty-eight, so I was told.

For such appointments — rare though they were — the two words that usually preceded or followed the name of the person was, "the first Negro..." During my unexpected, and somewhat miraculous, five-year tenure in the state of North Dakota, I saw those words often connected to my name in the various ventures the two jobs carried.

My family, old friends, and others in the Black community, would often squint their eyes, scratch their heads and smile when learning of my time out on the prairie. I would also hear them mutter...how could he possibly take such an assignment? By the time my second and third years arrived, they would boldly state, "How on earth did Bobby Polk manage to stay there so long and survive?"

Friends, former colleagues at the YMCA, and students with whom I have kept in touch, as well as those who, over sixty years, have heard the stories of what it was like to be out there, are often surprised. As one friend put it, "It was like being a reverse missionary: a Negro going to work with and among White people, rather than the opposite." A note to that effect, written in the Chicago Sun Times by a White friend, said what an anomaly this was. "Whites most often go to work, serve and 'help' Blacks, but not the other way around." I might as well have gone to Scandinavia or Germany for this assignment since ninety-nine percent of my work involved the Nordic population who came to North Dakota to open the territory, purchase the land and take ownership before, and soon after, it became a state in 1889.

I have never been a great raconteur, but I discovered that I can mesmerize an audience when given the opportunity to share my North Dakota tales. According to some, I can even match Garrison Keillor. When speaking to a seminary classmate recently, we both shared what kept us busy during the COVID lockdown. I told him of this project, and he immediately remembered one of my stories and repeated it, "A YMCA kid, with out-of-town friends, saw you coming down the street and one in the group shouted out, "Here comes a Nigger!" The little tow-headed Y member piped up and said, "That's not a Nigger. That's Bob Polk, our Y youth director and he is my friend."

What follows in these pages are anecdotes and interesting tales that speak of both the human condition experienced in the 1950's and, more importantly, how that Nordic community dealt with a Black man, me, and race relations prior to the formal civil rights movement as we knew it.

My life's work has moved along two parallel passions: ministry and social justice - majoring in race relations. You will learn later how this came about. More importantly, or, perhaps coincidently, by some strange quirk or coincidence, the result is that more than three quarters of my life and work has been almost exclusively with and among Caucasians. Recognizing this, I staked out my mission to help expose, educate, and inform White people about Black people, their life, culture, and humanity, with the hope of changing those lives and attitudes from negative to positive where necessary and whenever possible. I have been fortunate and blessed to keep these basic values in the forefront of every job I have been blessed and honored to have. These may be somewhat small incremental steps, but, nonetheless, they are steps in the right direction, and I can account for some progress in my work.

My way of helping White people getting to know Black folk — our history, culture, and life — is by sharing my personal story with roots that are deeply embedded in this nation's history and what we, as a people, have endured and contributed since our arrival as enslaved people in 1619. Hearts and minds are changed for the better when there is honest recognition of the truth. That is how our nation can become more inclusive and the beloved community we desire.

In ND my parishioners, friends, co-workers, youth leaders and others were either incurious, or race simply didn't matter. Few questions were asked or, when there was a new outbreak of lynching, civil rights unrest and so forth elsewhere, there was little discussion or opportunity for dialogue. The "why" of that continues to haunt and intrigue me. The absence of people of color meant that there was no frame of reference for the residents to even formulate the concept of race relations.

In this era of a toxic racial environment and the systemic racism we have known since 1619, my story is rather straightforward and somewhat of a period piece reflecting my years there, spreading positive race relations, accepting some of the slings and arrows of negativity expressed implicitly or explicitly, and trying to lead and educate by my example.

My YMCA work was, without a doubt, one of the most scintillating and enjoyable jobs I have experienced. To this day, whenever I think of my former teenagers, who are now in their mid-to-late seventies, it brings a smile, chuckle and a great glow to my very being. I recall them as a potpourri of typical teens: daring, bold, smart, funny, serious, arrogant, defiant, rebellious, loving, kind, generous, and compassionate.

I believe their ability to accept me came out of two directions. First, teens are open and accepting, based upon their independent thinking as well as peer pressure. Secondly, they loved feeling superior by having an experience their parents did not have. While their parents may have disapproved of my being the youth director at the Y, they could be proud of their values that differed so much from their parents and feel good about taking the high moral and social ground — for a change.

Many years after my sojourn in North Dakota, when I was executive of a prominent Child Care Agency in New York City, I was offered the opportunity to go to the far reaches of Maine with other executives on an Outward Bound experience deep within the wilderness. I accepted without knowing fully what Outward Bound entailed. Friends in the know warned me to think twice before going and that Outward Bound was a survival program similar to Boot Camp training in the military. After a second thought, I said to myself, "If I could survive five years in North Dakota, I could manage Outward Bound." So, I went and, may I add…barely survived!

The basic tenants of my Christian faith, my tenacity, work ethic, love of all sorts and conditions of people, resilience, a poor child of the Great Depression, willingness to sacrifice, and being Black with all its vicissitude, enabled me to share with others, learn to get along, and accept others by their commonality- humanity. It is those qualities and attributes that enabled me to survive in North Dakota and beyond.

All of this plays out on the pages ahead. I would be remiss if I did not take this space to thank several of my former Y co-workers/youth leaders, friends, and colleagues for not only fact checking, but for helping yours truly in memory checking. They know who they are, and I shall say more about them later.

RLP

Forword

I was fifteen when I met Robert Polk, the new Youth Minister at The Riverside Church in Manhattan. I called him 'my oldest living friend,' and he still is. I became one of a burgeoning number of young people who turned to Bob over many decades for mentoring, honest answers about life and a broadening of our experience and perspective. Throughout the years, I have watched myriad and diverse groups of young and old stay connected to him despite geographical and generational differences, recognizing his outstanding qualities as a leader and guide and drawn to his enormous capacity for friendship, loyalty and abiding love.

This book is about the first experiences he had in his ministry of over sixty-five years, in North Dakota, in the mid-1950s. For many in the community, Bob was the first Black person they had ever seen or met. To this day, many of the teenagers he helped nurture in Berthold and Minot still call, write and visit him in his retirement community in Philadelphia. Some of his unusual history was serendipitous or providential; in other cases, he was able to see possibilities and went out to meet them. His uncommon story, which continues in his nineties, in some ways reflects much of the social changes of the era, involving race relations, social justice issues and multiculturalism, but always revolving around his faith, unique personality, and a blend of curiosity, openness, and optimism.

After Minot, Bob Polk became the first Black Youth Minister, later Urban Affairs Minister at Riverside Church, among many 'firsts,' as well as Dean of Students at Dillard University during the turbulent sixties, Executive Director of the New York City Council of Churches, Trustee at City University of New York (CUNY) and many other interim positions. He served on many boards and committees, including the New York Urban League, the Alvin Ailey Dance Theatre, the World Alliance of Reformed Churches and the Albert Schweitzer Fellowship. During those years he took on multiple and varied undertakings, such as establishing the first HIV/AIDS program in New York City, founding the Prison Ministry at Riverside Church, and hosting powerful world leaders like Bishop Tutu, the King of Spain, and the Dalai Lama, yet was strongly connected to the struggling and the disinherited. He spoke and preached in cathedrals as well as small, regular, and storefront churches. After retirement he established The Robert L. Polk lectureship on race and social justice at Doane University, his Alma Mater in Nebraska, an ongoing Black Arts Festival in his Philadelphia, ninety-nine percent White, retirement community. He has written two books, and founded a barbershop quartet in which he sings. His strong faith, deep African American roots, and generosity of spirit have led and guided him throughout his life, as he built bridges between those who did not know one another yet and taught us to trust, care, and believe in inclusiveness for all people, moving towards that much sought after Beloved Community.   .

Cecile Terrien-Lampton

Part I

"We would be building temples still undone
O'er crumbling walls their crosses scarcely lift,
Waiting till love can raise the broken stone,
And hearts creative bridge the human rift.
We would be building, Master, let thy plan
Reveal the life that God would give to man."
                                    - Purd E. Deitz

"Where cross the crowded ways of life,
Where sound the cries of race and clan,
Above the noise of selfish strife,
We hear thy voice, O Son of man."
                                    - Frank Mason

"Fly in the Buttermilk"
One Black man's odyssey out on the Prairie

Whenever asked to give a brief biographical rundown, either in a focus group or a larger arena, I follow the traditional protocol. Telling audiences of being born during the Great Depression on the South Side of racially toxic and highly segregated Chicago. Stating that I was the youngest of six children to loving, struggling parents, and the descendent of enslaved grandparents. I move on to say that, in today's language, my family would be considered members of the "working poor" class. My father, a laborer, worked thirty-seven years for a major company, and never missed a day's work. He trained three of his White co-workers to be his boss and earned one fourth of their pay. Each of my siblings and I started to work at the age of twelve to help support our home and family. We learned early on of the dignity and importance of work. I then would cut to the chase in a "getting to know you" exercise and move on to my North Dakota playbook; chronicling my years and work there. At this point, I can always count on one member of my audience to call out, "You mean South Dakota!" Correction! "No, I mean North Dakota."

Often in break-out sessions, or some other down-time, one or two curious dear souls will push me for further details and more information regarding this Black man in a lily-white state out on the Great Plains that few people knew about. At which point I speak of the city of Minot, the fourth largest city in the state, in its northwest, close to the Canadian border. Minot's population, during my tenure (1957 – 1960), was about 35,000, with a predominantly Scandinavian, German, and other Northern European ancestry. If my questioners want me to go deeper about my work in that environment and how I managed to work there as a YMCA Youth

Program Secretary, I take them to another level — the underbelly of that community and how it supported a thriving red-light district for many years, known as Third Street. The jaw-dropping, OMG convulsion comes when I reveal the fact that most of the "ladies of the night" on Third Street were African Americans in this otherwise all White community.

Since the publication of my memoir in 2013, which described one of the most varied and extraordinary ministries this African American pastor could possibly have had, friends have often asked me to focus on a few of my stories and tell them in more detail and include insights that I have had over the years. They wish to know how I managed to fulfill these assignments, especially as it relates to the issues of race and social justice, that inevitably arose. Fly in the Buttermilk is the result of my attempt to satisfy my questioners and, in the process, to think once more about how my life has been shaped by my early ministries. Because I procrastinate as much as anyone when it comes to taxing my memory and settling down to work, revisiting my early days and putting my thoughts and reflections on paper has been both long and personally rewarding.

My first attempt to write about my uncommon experiences resulted in a paper, "Bearer of the Tale." There I share my short two-year tenure, 1966 – 1968, as Dean of Chapel and Dean of Students at Dillard University, a Historically Black University in New Orleans, Louisiana.

The present attempt reflects on an earlier period of my career, my five years in the state of North Dakota, from 1955 — 1960, and how these two accounts are at both ends of the social spectrum. This memoir shows how a Black man lived, worked and kept his sanity in such personal contrasts, not to mention those in-between job assignments.

During all of this, the issue of my parallel calling and passions allowed me to keep focused — pastoring and fighting for social justice — as it relates to improving race relations wherever I landed, leaving my mark.

As Covid-19 gripped our country and a lockdown was mandated, especially in the retirement community in which I live, I was drawn back to this writing project that had been marinating in my mind over the past sixty years. Perhaps the account was a sign? That now was the time to devote to sharing my story of being a single Black man, living, working, and embedded (for five years) in the state of North Dakota, and the issues of both race and survival that arise.

My mind became packed, even restless, with extraordinary reflections and memories of those bygone years. Believe me, not many months or years have passed that I don't think about my work there. And, better yet, that is underscored by former teenagers and friends who have kept me tuned in over the years with emails, cards, letters, visits, and phone calls from that very rich and exciting experience.

Now that I have settled on this, my Covid – 19 project, pulling out artifacts, photos, notes and letters, plus putting my long-term memory to work in overdrive, a strange thing happened. Perhaps it was a sign that I should get serious, clamp down and consciously make this my cardinal project during the pandemic. A most unusual thing occurred; A remarkable docu-ment arrived in the mail. Upon opening, I read, "Why Minot," a report written by the Minot Junior Chamber of Commerce, a well-researched, written, and engaging document chronicling Minot's long closeted, seldom spoken of, but highly flourishing, organized prostitution and the dark cloud of vice and criminality that cast a pall over the city.

Though written and compiled in 1960, it was researched, assembled, and distributed to business, church and civic leaders throughout the community. All of this happened after my departure from Minot in the fall of 1960. Had I remained, I am sure my opinion would have been requested along with the esteemed business, clergy, and other professional leaders in the city. I was flabbergasted, especially by the propitious time of its arrival. It certainly made me feel as though I had received a sliver of a refresher course on Minot as I commenced my writing.

Without placing a value judgement on the document, I, as an African American, must give high marks to the JC. In all its pages of facts and figures, they refrained from mentioning that half to a majority of the women in this Third Street operation were African American. I shall return to the Third Street phenomenon several times in this account and how it interlaced within the community of all White people (men) and who were the clients, johns, benefactors, and stakeholders. The hypocrisy that gripped the town regarding this social cancerous enigma, was something no one wanted to speak of, yet was difficult to ignore.

I trace my social activism back to my early teens in Chicago, which had a legacy of racism and was one of the worst for a northern city of its size. In all ages, racial bias seemed to be a topic on everyone's agenda. Our community, West Woodlawn, was like a little island, surrounded by Whites on all four sides. Racial skirmishes, riots, restrictive covenants, and other issues kept the races divided, during the time that the Great Migration was in full swing. Negroes were coming in large numbers, needing places to live, work, spread out and have that sense of "freedom" they had been promised before leaving the south. All of this was difficult to come by.

West Woodlawn was in its early days part of White flight. Blacks started moving in from Bronzeville, where many Negroes lived. However, West Woodlawn was controlled by Whites, meaning they were the merchants, social workers, public health officials and even street cleaners, postal de-livery men, shop owners, schoolteachers, police and more. Thus, interac-tion was not always at its best and Negroes, in all reality, were powerless and had little to say about their community and how it operated.

Negro women often worked as domestics in either the border White communities or those ultra-rich places north of the Loop or places like South Shore. Newly developing ethnic communities, inhabited largely by immigrants, were, even as newcomers, actively anti-Black. There was sel-dom a dinner table gathering in my home, and most others, where race did not make the agenda. This was almost always in a negative tone; we dis-cussed what the White folk were doing to us, usually with first-hand stories as evidence.

During all of this in the early 1940's, my family (originally Baptist) became members of the Congregational Christian Church. There were only two Negro Congregational Churches in Chicago and over seventy White ones. Our new minister and his wife were standouts at a time when the Congregational denomination, nationally and locally, set out to try to live the social gospel. New policies were established decrying racism and pro-claiming brotherhood, tolerance, and better under-standing among Negroes in general and from its two Congrega-tional Churches in particular.

My church, the first Negro Congregational Church in the city, was Lincoln Memorial Church, established in 1904. I became a member of our church's youth group, Pilgrim Fellowship (PF), which emphasized social action, race relations, and political action. Pilgrim Fellowship also had a strong commitment to the basic tenets of the Christian faith. I soon became its president. Being Black at a time when the Congregational church was focusing on race, I soon rose through the ranks of our city, state, and na-tional Christian youth initiative. And that was the beginning of my life of becoming "the first" Negro in one thing and then another. At a time when my unacceptable school behavior was almost off the charts and was begin-ning to show delinquent patterns, it was through this church program that I channeled my energy and attention towards working with other youth and clergy to achieve a better society, devoid of racism and more. My minister's wife, Mrs. Eleanor Rush, engaged me in reading and caring more about Negro history, especially that which had been left out of traditional history books, and in keeping up with contemporary books about the Negro race. I found myself almost withdrawing from my old friends as I was engaging with so many White people; We tried to understand the social gospel and how it affected our lives, homes, families and churches. I had given in to all this race and multicultural talk and action, but not without questioning its viability. Was I deserting my lifelong friends? And was it worth moving in and among White church cohorts? This was my per-sonal dilemma.

Returning home one Sunday for family dinner, following one of those mountain-top experiences, as my family gathered around the Sunday din-ner table, I sensed a change in the tone and tenor of my siblings' conver-sation. Finally, it came out. The discussion was, how could I possibly get involved with all those White people, knowing what they have done and continue to do to us? A heated discussion ensued regarding Black/White relations, bringing up our experiences with them in our community.

Whites were racists, bigots, prejudiced and unkind and indifferent to Blacks. Our community was controlled by Whites. My family knew I was aware of the tensions between Blacks and Whites throughout the city and especially in our communities. We were limited, almost enslaved, by the boundaries set up by White folk. Thus, when my dinner table family coun-cil took on my hobnobbing with White people, they were both trying to protect me from being hurt and letting me know the real deal, as they un-derstood it, about White people. One of the statements we had in my com-munity regarding our disdain for White people was, "We don't do White people" ...And that was one of the more polite phrases.

Thus, my family let me know that they did not want to see me get hurt and be diminished by whoever those White folks were that demanded so much of my time. I made my somewhat feeble defense regarding the Church, Christianity, love of God and Jesus and the idea that all people were created equal and more. By the end of dessert, my beloved oldest sis-ter, Lois, the one who was my caregiver in my toddling years and more, who always saw the good side of life, summarized it by laughing and saying, "you must look like a fly in the buttermilk in all of those White gatherings". My friends, too, questioned me about being associated with a White church. They too grumbled, but their disdain was less polite than my fam-ily's cautions.

Weeks later, my mother took me aside and told me the story of Roland Hayes, one of our world-renowned Negro tenors. During his first European tour, he performed a concert before the Queen of England and her family. In his excitement, he wired his mother and gave her the good news. She immediately wired back with these words: "Never forget who you are and whose you are." I got the message from my mother, and it has followed me over the years.

Remembrances and reflections crowd my mind as I write about this part of my past in more detail and describe how I became embedded for a lifetime among White people. I realized that I might be able to have an im-pact on some of their lives and possibly help them to become more sensi-tive, tolerant, and empathetic in their views and practices as we strove together for racial equality and justice for my people. My involvement was both with the church and with social action groups and organizations as they emerged over the years. I found my greatest opportunities to help change lives through individual and small group encounters rather than larger civil rights organizations.

I was no stranger to North Dakota, the northernmost and least under-stood state of the Great Plains. Before I became its official forty-eighth Negro resident in 1955, I had visited the state on three other occasions. Join me in this journey, with special attention related to race.

Summer of 1947 – Pilgrim Fellowship was a weeklong Congregational Church summer youth camp for teenagers in the Turtle Mountains on Lake

Metigoshe, on the Canadian border. I boarded the CB&Q train, the "Empire Builder," on the Great Northern railroad in Chicago's Union Station at about four in the afternoon and arrived in Minot, ND, at five the following morning. Little did I realize that within a few years, that train, The Empire Builder, would become my regular mode of transport between Chicago and Minot. Coincidently, after college years, I landed a job as a dining car waiter on the CB&Q, hoping to see the westernmost part of country it served while I earned enough money to attend seminary. Unfortunately, my assignment never took me to the end of the route in Seattle, WA. That's another story.

On this occasion, the national leadership team of my denomination's youth program, Pilgrim Fellowship, dispersed its officers to attend summer camps and conferences around the country to talk up Pilgrim Fellowship and to work at helping Junior and Senior high school students and their leaders, to take on social action, political action and faith-based spirituality. The goal was to help bring about better understanding and relationships between Blacks and Whites. One of my assignments was the North Dakota camp.

I landed in Minot on time and met one of the camp counselors, who was also pastor of the Minot Congregational Church. We went to his church where, later that morning, I was to meet a contingent of teenagers and their counselors to travel by bus up to Lake Metigoshe. This was my first exposure to the state of North Dakota, and it all seemed quite foreign to me. I really cannot recall ever having heard anything about the state before that. I soon realized that the students, and the clergy who were their leaders, were all White and came from tiny towns and villages throughout this agrarian state. I also discovered that most were of Scandinavian, German and of other Northern European heritage and had attended the one room schoolhouses and quaint little white clapboard churches that dotted the landscape of the region. And, of greater importance, they had never seen or been close to a Black person before, even though the adults, lay and clergy tried to act otherwise. My work was cut out for me!

These tow-headed youngsters, for the most part, were curious, mystified, awestruck and not sure whether to get close or keep their distance. Once they settled down and enjoyed some small group sessions, meals, singing, formally addressing the group and more, the gloves came off. They touched my skin to see if it rubbed off, felt my hair, peppered me with questions about my home, my family, how it felt to be Black, and asked if I was from Africa. By the time we broke camp, they could return home and tell their families, school chums, and teachers not only about the Christian gospel and mission of Jesus, but about the Negro (I hope they used "Negro") they had met at summer camp. And, no doubt, essays were written that fall when they returned to school about their unusual summer experience – all of which was to the good. How I would have enjoyed reading some of their statements.

Summer 1948
The Great Hitchhiking Expedition
From Chicago To Saskatachewan, Canada

Doug Kelley and I met at a church youth retreat at Chicago Theological Seminary, at the University of Chicago, in 1944. The focus was on social and political action. Doug was from that wealthy White section of Chicago known as South Shore. He was well-read and deeply into politics, and we struck up a lifelong friendship. Doug had a great influence on me and guided me to join him in adding activism to my church involvement.

During those early high school years, I was enamored with social activities and events Doug introduced me to that I was unaware of in the Black community, such as tobogganing, square dancing, hiking out in the Forest Preserves and more. Some of my dates were not so enthusiastic with such activities, but I took to them.

He first attended Michigan State University, I believe. I went a few blocks south of my high school to Wilson Junior College. Higher education was not in my plans as I was to be drafted into the army, the day following my high school graduation. Doug and I kept in touch and double dated whenever he was in Chicago and carried on our involvement in social and political activities, marches, demonstrations, workshops, and conferences. One highlight was attending a rally at Chicago Coliseum sponsored by the great A. Philip Randolph when he first announced his March on Washington idea for jobs. Randolph was a civil rights worker and union organizer. He organized the successful Brotherhood of Sleeping Car Porters which was extraordinarily important for Negro men who worked on the railroad. We joined the Americans for Democratic Action (ADA) and attended its first convention near the University of Chicago. We also visited the new CORE Fellowship House when it opened in the Windy City.

Our studies, though at different schools, had opened our eyes to the progressive politics of the upper northwest with its cooperatives, the Farm Labor Movement, and other liberal contributions from that Scandinavian dotted land. Hubert Humphrey was Mayor of Minneapolis and Henry Wallace was on the horizon to run for president of the United States, following his VP tenure with FDR. We helped form a cadre of teens from our Congrega-

Two Helstrom kids on a farm in Saskatachewan, Canada

tional Churches of Chicago to work more closely together in social action and met twice a month taking on a few major projects for our age group which we thought helped make a difference. Our name was The Disciples for Christian Action (DCA). On one occasion, Doug had set up an appointment with Norman Thomas for an interview Doug was to write up for his school's newspaper. Norman Thomas was a socialist and six-time presidential candidate for the USA. Though I could not join him, I patiently waited at a nearby drug store, sipping a coke waiting for Doug to return. According to Doug, it was a smashing success!

It was during this time frame that I returned home one evening and found my parents distraught. As they explained it, earlier that evening, an FBI agent had paid a visit to them. He was inquiring about my attendance at a particular event and my support of Henry Wallace for president. It was not in my parents' DNA for their son to be in trouble with the Chicago Police Department (not to mention FBI) and they asked me to tone down my activities. Although they had appreciated my fight in the struggle for racial justice, they were concerned for my wellbeing. With that being said, I followed their wishes. There were no more visits from the FBI.

Hitchhiking — summer of 1948

In the summer of 1948, Doug came up with the idea of hitchhiking to Saskatchewan, Canada which, he said, had the only socialist government in North America. As naive as I tended to be about some of those things, that did not mean much to me. I truly believe Doug got the idea from his visit with Norman Thomas. At any rate, he encouraged me to join him, indicating that this would probably be our last summer when we could be free to do as we wished. I had been counseling at a church camp in Northern Wisconsin, where Doug met me and we took off for Canada.

We had about six weeks and less than fifty dollars each, as I recall. This was to be a totally new experience for me, but I think Doug had hitchhiked before, on a limited basis, and furthermore, hitchhiking was one means of travel and seeing other parts of the country. No Interstate Highways back then. We opted to take the scenic route up through towns and villages, along with much of the mythology, for example, Paul Bunyan in Wisconsin and into the 10,000-land o' lakes state of Minnesota, taking in all that we could along the way. Rides were better some days than others; however, downpours of rain, blazing summer temperatures, and giant mosquitoes were obviously impediments for these city slickers. Plus, we had our times of disagreement and self-imposed silence. The two things I absolutely refused to do were to hop a freight train when car rides had dried up. I was not about to become a hobo. And, secondly, I refused to sleep out under the stars at night in some farmer's hayfield.

Once we finally reached the USA/Canadian border in Minnesota, we presented our credentials to a friendly USA border guard, but his counterpart on the Canadian side was not very friendly. The border stations were run by the national government and our mission to visit Saskatchewan and its socialist government simply did not fly with the guard. Plus, we had little cash and the guard felt we might become wards of the country. In addition, the fact that we were Black and White didn't help matters. He turned us down and we hightailed it back to our USA buddy who understood the situation perfectly well. He suggested that since our goal was Saskatchewan, we hitchhike west in the USA and cross into Canada at North Portal, North Dakota, – "The Peace Garden State." We took his advice and headed west along the border to North Dakota, where I had been that previous summer… though under more pleasant circumstances. Both money (and at times, tempers) were growing fragile, but we made it through ND, and I arrived for the second time into the city of Minot. It was a name we spent considerable time quibbling over how to pronounce. Finally, one of our rides helped us out with pronouncing Minot. He simply said this catch phrase, "Why not, Minot" and it stuck. There was nothing special about Minot and we kept going.

We reached North Portal and went through the same process as we had in Minnesota—a great reception on the USA side, but an indignant turn-down at the Canadian outpost for some of the same reasons we encountered in Minnesota.

By now it was evening. We noticed a rundown, shabby roadhouse. We took a room and had breakfast the next morning. Doug got on the phone to the Regina Cooperative Commonwealth Federation - CCF headquarters and explained our plight. As luck would have it, their MP (member of parliament) was in town, and they spoke with him on our behalf. He, in turn, called the border guard and insisted that we be allowed to enter. And, by the next morning, we had a call at the roadhouse which Doug took, and all was hunky-dory. That same guard could not have been more pleasant as he welcomed us to Canada.

The border official explained to us that North Dakota was known as The Peace Garden State because The Sioux Nation, in so many negotiations and contacts with the U.S. government, felt, for the most part, it was acting in good faith, whatever the issue was. The Sioux people and their leaders called this Northwest Territory "The Peace Garden State." This vast area brought together friends and allies when the Sioux Nation negotiated and carried out official business with the people of North Dakota. They were fond, in poetic terms, of the enormous plains and rolling hills. There is majesty in the skies during the day and in the stars of the night.

This was an appropriate description that helped us to view the trek before us, rather than just seeing the endless prairie on the Canadian side.

Another issue between Doug and me was, he wanted to hitchhike up to Regina, and I simply refused, always thinking about race, and not knowing much about Canada in that regard. I did not need to have problems in a foreign country, so far from home and my people and nearly out of cash. We took the bus – we were a few bucks poorer but, what the heck, we rode in style and comfort and slept through the entire trip across more prairie and flat land. What was there to see?

We landed in Regina in the afternoon, headed for the YMCA, booked a room, cleaned up, grabbed a sandwich, and headed out to see this, our first Canadian city, our first trip north of the 49-degree parallel.

We headed for the provincial capital building. As we climbed up a long bank of stairs, a man coming down, carrying what appeared to be documents under his arm, smiled as we continued upward. Doug nudged me

and said, "Bob, I think that's T.C. Douglas, the premier of the province, whose likeness/photo was on the Saskatchewan Map. I shrugged, and before I could say anything, Doug called out, "Mr. Douglas." The man turned around and, sure 'nuff, it was he.

He stopped, smiled again, and we introduced ourselves. He was delighted to meet us and learn about our mission and where we hailed from. He shifted his papers and engaged us in conversation, informing us that he had once lived in Chicago and attended the Divinity School at the University of Chicago. Later we discovered he had been a Baptist minister before his career in politics.

That short, engaging meeting led Mr. Douglas to tell us of the CCF's Provincial convention, starting Sunday in the city of Saskatoon. Furthermore, he said, if we were interested, we could ride along with him and get a larger picture of the CCF, the convention, and meet the youth contingent of the party. All of which floored us. But we agreed. Doug, always the bolder one of us, agreed first, and then I followed suit.

There we were, two grungy teenage American hitchhikers, about to have one of the treats of our lives: riding with the Premier of the province and taking in his annual convention in a city we had never heard of.

Premier Douglas agreed to pick us up at the YMCA at a certain time on Sunday morning. He would be the driver, unlike a US Governor lounging behind their chauffeur. We looked at ourselves and smiled, remembering we were without decent clothing to make such a trip. Saturday evening, we scouted around Regina and found a men's clothing store whose name I shall never forget — Wear's Ware Wears Well. We went in and found shirts and trousers, which dug seriously into our shrinking budget, purchased them and returned to the Y.

The next morning, we skimped on breakfast, lollygagged around the lobby, hoping some of the residents would be there when the premier came calling. This did not happen. He was late and we waited a long time before he arrived. Once he did, we had grown hungry and tired, again!

We spent the couple of hours as we headed north to Saskatoon getting to know Mr. Douglas and vice versa. Doug did most of the talking on our end. Mr. Douglas had informed us earlier that he had to make one stop at a small, rural town, to dedicate a newly built twenty bed hospital. A few miles out, we were met by two Canadian Mounties who hailed Mr. Douglas' car, chatted, and escorted him – us – into the town in high style! The area surrounding the hospital was crowded with many adults and their children. When Mr. Douglas was called upon to speak, he was indeed charismatic and fiery in his delivery. Some even commented that he was like William Jennings Bryan. Following the dedicatory ceremony, he was invited to stay for supper. He told the chairman he had two Americans with him. That was okay and we too were invited for supper. And eat we did!

We continued to Saskatoon, met again by another set of Mounties who escorted the premier to his hotel where the convention was to be held. At this point, Mr. Douglas made sure we were introduced to the youth contingent of the CCF. We spent the remainder of the convention with them, where what we learned about CCF, and its strength in that one province, made us wish for it to become more widely accepted in the whole country.

At the close of the convention, we lucked out on a ride back to Regina where we had hopes of landing two weeks of work to earn enough to get us back to the USA and home.

One great scene off in the distance caught our eyes. What seemed like thousands of Native Canadians were holding a celebration with dancing, tepees, food and more. We were told by our driver that it was the time of the year for the annual gathering of several tribes.

Once back in Regina, we hightailed it to the employment office to see if someone might give us work. It was now late August and close to harvest time. We filed our papers, looking gaunt, pitiful, and poor – which we were—with few, if any, skills needed by farmers in the area. As the good Lord would have it, one guy kept looking at us and finally came up to introduce himself as Paul Helstrom. He was looking for farm laborers and wondered who we were and what our skills were. Needless to say, we were without any skills he needed. However, this Good Samaritan had pity on us and said he would take us to his farm, put us up, and see if he could find some menial labor for the days we had left in Canada.

We arrived at his farm and home, met his wife, two teenage daughters and younger son. We were in luck. Dinner was ready and we all ate together.

Mr. Helstrom pushed barnyard chores our way, cleaning the slough, the icehouse, raking, tidying up the area, and other chores. He had built a bunk house for farm laborers, which was where we ended up staying. The oldest daughter immediately had a crush on Doug. I can't recall what we earned, but it was sufficient for our time there with this wonderful family with whom we continued to stay in touch years later. On the day of my ordination in 1955, I received a package from Gray, Saskatchewan, Canada. It was a Revised Standard Version (RSV) of the Holy Bible. I still have and cherish it!

Heading back home, we had enough to cover our meager needs. When we reached the middle of Wisconsin, we planned to split and go our separate ways, and we did. Doug went over to Madison, to a youth political action weekend conference sponsored by the AFL/CIO at the University of Wisconsin. While I hitched over to Green Lake to a Church Vocations Conference for high school and college students interested in the Christian ministry. That was a metaphor for this duo's long friendship.

It took seven rides for me to reach Green Lake, I must admit there was anxiety on how I was to manage hitchhiking as a single Black man. One of the interesting caveats is that of the seven rides, three of the drivers immediately discussed the sexual genital differences between Black men and White men. Each of those men attempted to grope me. I soon realized that I needed to keep my duffle bag on my lap.

Doug went on to become a skilled, sharp, insightful political science major and activist with several degrees. He was also a consultant to Democratic political figures in Michigan. Doug also graduated from Berea College and went on to achieve advanced degrees from the University of Michigan and J.F.K School of Government. While at Berea, I believe, he collected a group of students to go to Saskatchewan and study CCF. They too met Premier T.C. Douglas (Doug said he asked about me). He ended up buying and selling political archives and antiques specializing in Vice Presidents of the U.S. and other collectables. Ultimately, he had such an important collection that he built a museum on his own property in Ann Arbor, MI. In all his political career and given his expertise, Doug was a high-level political consultant to Michigan Democratic politicians and beyond.

Doug was a household name in our home. He often visited or would call via phone. My mother kept a foster child, named Cathy. Whenever she answered the phone from Doug, she could not get his name right and would say, Bobby, Slug called.

On another level, Doug with his gift of gab, ability to convince and challenge most people, met his match when it came to my mother. He was my only White friend who engaged my mother in racial and political arguments – dialogue. Mother was also well read and kept up with local and national events via reading the Chicago Tribune, and so forth. She and my father were Lincoln Republicans/not Democrats from enslaved parents and more. Doug, of course was an FDR Democrat, a liberal free thinker. Mother would not allow him to get away with too much, and especially when it came to race and social injustice against Negroes. She would draw upon experiences in her youth in Georgia happening upon a failed lynching, Jim Crow, KKK, White terrorism, and would speak about peonage, sharecropping, some of my father's experiences, especially scrimping and saving enough money to help one of my father's brothers come to Chicago from Texas. He arrived, lived with us, found a job with a circus. It was going into southern Illinois and beyond, according to his report. From the day he left, they never heard from him again. Probably a lynching or whatever. So, Doug could never out talk my mother when it came to race in America. He would join us for dinner following such discussions and we broke bread about the table and enjoyed the company.

Doug Kelley was my friend, all through the years, since we first met when we were both 14 years old. As you will learn elsewhere in this memoir, our paths paralleled each other in working to make positive changes in society through active engagement in confronting prejudice and racism by promoting civil rights. I like to joke that he was my oldest White friend! From early on, we marched, picketed, and demonstrated together way back in the mid-40s.

That's why I am so delighted to say that Doug had an illustrious professional career and, most significantly, created the International Development Placement Association that sent committed young Americans abroad to perform service work. The effort became quite popular, and hundreds applied to take part. Doug's concept, proven feasible, was endorsed by Hubert Humphrey, who introduced legislation to create the Peace Corp, inaugurated by President John F. Kennedy. Yes, my friend created the Peace Corp! It is no wonder that I have held him in such high esteem for his searching mind, commitment to working in the margins and his devotion to making the world a better place.

It was extremely difficult to bring closure to a strong, hail and hearty friendship that lasted some eighty years when he died. In all these years, Doug and I had kept in touch. That meant personal visits, family visits, NYC visits and especially Broadway Theater trips. I shall never forget the year 1952, when the Democratic National Convention met in Chicago, Doug was a delegate from Michigan. He made sure I had a ticket one night down on the floor along with his fellow delegates. That was the year that Adlai Stevenson was nominated. Every DNC convention, thereafter, my long term memory kicks in and I am reminded of the 1952 experience which I have always cherished.

I lost contact with Doug about three years ago when I had no information about the retirement community in which he lived or contact informa-tion about his son Peter. I so much wanted to share the Doug Kelley part of this memoir with him for old times' sake as well as memory checking. All to no avail. However, during my last days of writing, I had a call from his son, Peter Kelley, informing me of Doug's death back in January 2022. I was honored to be asked to say a few words at the memorial service on May 7, and I did, though with some technical difficulties. Again, this was one of the longest, continual friendships in my life and, as you can tell, my mem-ories of the Douglas Kelley are strong and abiding! He and I remained close throughout the years.

When I learned of his death from his son Peter, I came to the realization of what an impact Doug had on my life. When I speak in the memoir about my vocation and its parallel lines, one as pastor and the second in social justice and race relations, I have been fortunate to combine these forces in all that I have done. Only now do I realize how much of this second part I owe to Doug Kelley, for which I will always be eternally grateful, especially now that I have identified from whence it cameMy memories of the Douglas Christian Kelley are strong and abiding!

Rest In Peace, good buddy!

While Doug followed his own path, I, on the other hand, kept my social activism within the confines of the Congregational denomination. I entered a Congregational Church related-college, Doane College in Nebraska and, following graduation, took a year off to work and earn money that would enable me to attend Hartford Theological Seminary in Connecticut.

1953
Garrison, North Dakota
Summer Student Intern (Crisis & Opportunity)

At the close of one's first year in seminary, students were expected to work through the Field Work office and land a summer intern job. The point was that hopefully assisting a seasoned pastor and learning some of the ecclesiastical tricks of the trade (while earning a salary in the process or pastoring a small, mostly rural church) and learning immeasurably from that experience would enhance one's pastorate for years to come. My small Chicago Congregational Church could not afford to hire me, and I was open to employment elsewhere. A handful of my fellow students were headed to parishes in North Dakota. They suggested I meet with the Conference Minister of the state (Rev. Edward Treat) to see if there was a church out there for me. I met with Rev. Treat, and he reviewed my seminary work and other credentials. Again, the denomination was focused on improving race relations and Rev. Treat did not have a Black church nor a Black member in a church in his state. However, the interview went well, and my fellow students were most supportive. Rev. Treat said he would look around and inquire to see if any of his churches would be willing to bring on a Black student.

Surprise! He contacted me a few weeks later and offered me a job in the small town of Garrison, ND, where I would assist the current pastor and live in the parsonage with the pastor, his wife, and young daughter.

It was fine with me. However, he hinted that the stakes were high and that there was some friction in the church over his recommendation they take a Negro in their parish and town.

It was not until I arrived, settled in with Rev. Frank Hirons, his wife

Dorothy, and Nancy (their five-year-old daughter), that I was made aware of just how divisive and fractious my coming was among the congregation and the town.

When Rev. Treat first approached my coming through the church officers, the Deacons and Trustees were fine, but insisted the matter be taken up at a congregational meeting. As the word got out, members of the congregation began to take sides. That turned into a story that I have cherished and used multiple times in sermons; referencing as to how one person can make a difference at a critical juncture in the life of the church — or elsewhere.

Hazel McElwain's story goes like this:

At the congregational meeting, the one item on the agenda was whether to call me. Rev. Treat informed me that the discussion became heated. However, the minister and his wife and many others were all quite positive about my coming. When the vote was called, it was half and half. One of the members who held her vote said she wanted to make a statement before casting her vote that would break the tie.

Hazel told the congregation that during WWII, her husband was drafted into the service. She was left with two young children to care for. During the dark days of that period, she became involved in a Pen Pal program in which an American selected a person in Europe of similar background, and they corresponded during the war. This provided good therapy, bonding, and friendship on both sides of the Atlantic.

Hazel's friend lived in a small town in France, and she had two children the same age as Hazel's. At one point, her village had been taken over by the Germans, who ravaged and nearly destroyed the town. Later, the Americans came in, defeated the Germans, and took control of the town. She described how wonderful the U.S. occupying troops were; how they helped to clean up the town, fix vital arteries, work with families on home repairs, and more. The last thing she said was that these U.S. troops were Negroes. She closed by saying to Hazel that they saved their lives, but that the troops also often spoke about the racial segregation and discrimination they faced when they returned home. Finally, she said to Hazel, if you ever have a chance to do something good for Negroes in your country, do it for me and my village. It would mean so much to us.

Well, Hazel voted to break the tie for me to come to Garrison. Rev. Treat and most of the congregation were pleased. This demonstrates how one person can and did make a difference!

Another story I was told concerned one of the pillars of the church (who was opposed to my coming). He withdrew his family membership and made a call on the Lutheran pastor requesting to join his church. The wise Lutheran pastor had heard of the Congregational Church's dilemma and vote. When the disaffected member explained why he wished to join the Lutheran church, the pastor said if that was his reason, the Lutheran church would not accept him for membership either!

That was the social/racial climate in which I was to work for two months. In the first month, I would be working in conjunction with the pastor; a teaching and mentoring experience regarding the key elements of pastoring. During the second month, Rev. Hirons and his family would be on vacation, and I would be in charge.

Here I was, the "fly" again. Completely unhinged and totally unsure of what to expect in what could have been a toxic environment for me. Whom could I expect to be friends or otherwise? Up and down the streets, would I be taunted when walking along? Who would show up for church and more? This was the first time I had been confronted with a moral situation and what to do about it. Would the summer be dodging slurs with no friendly, smiling folk? And what about the young people in the Pilgrim Fellowship I was to mentor? I was not about to give up, but I did have early, demanding days and moments of curiosity that gave me pause for deep reflection on race and personal interactions.

Without keeping you in suspense, you will be delighted to know that by the end of my term, things could not have been better! As parochial as the teens of the church and community could have been, they stepped up and made me feel welcomed, giving their all to our summer Pilgrim Fellowship (youth) initiative.

There was even one interracial couple and family with teens in my program. The father was Native American, and the mother was Caucasian. The father was from the nearby Ft. Berthold Indian Reservation and, whenever the family went out to the reservation for special events and celebrations, they invited me to go along. I even encountered two young Indian girls from our Congregational mission church whom I had met at a national Pilgrim Fellowship youth rally a few years earlier. They could not have been more welcoming, along with their families.

Also on the reservation were our denomination's missionaries, Rev. and Mrs. Harold (Eva) Case. They were salt of the earth people to the reservation, where they had been for over forty years, as strong advocates for the Indian community. They were the "go to" folk from the Tribal Council down to families and individuals, all of whom depended on the Case's.

That summer they hosted a Work Camp for college students from around the country, amounting to about twenty of all races. I interacted with them and spent a few evenings with them at the end of the day and was awe-struck listening to their stories, along with their peers from the reservation, around the campfire singing church and folk songs. Such Kum Ba Yah moments were rich bonding experiences of sharing and getting to know each other.

One family, with two teenaged daughters, the Landsedels – as I recall - in my youth group, had a brother in the military, soon to be home on furlough. The family, and especially his sisters, had written about me and he was anxious to get to know me. We spent two afternoons along the Missouri River at one of his favorite spots. It was here he spent hours as a youth digging around searching for Indian arrowheads. We tried, to no avail, but we did go skinny dipping in the big muddy Missouri, and he assured me I was probably the first Negro to swim in this part of the river. Before he returned to camp, he presented me with two of his arrowheads. Unfortunately, I misplaced them in my many moves during my career.

All this joy and excitement in a place I thought would be a bust, and more, increased my summer from my expectations to a joyous reality.

I was without a car and had to walk every place in town, especially when Rev. Hirons was on vacation. One hot morning, I received a call from the local hospital. It was a nurse, a member of my church. But we had not met. She reported that I was the only cleric in town and that she had an emergency that needed a minister.

At issue was that one of her patients who had delivered a breach baby that morning. The baby was not expected to live and the mother was not doing well. Would I come down to the hospital and baptize the baby? I had not performed that sacrament. That is what summer internship was all about, I assume. I tidied myself up, went into Rev. Heron's daughter's room and picked out a doll, pulled out the worship handbook for the denomination, went to the kitchen sink and practiced.

When I arrived at the hospital, shirt, and tie ready, the nurse greeted me and took me into the incubation room. She gingerly lifted the baby, held it, and I did the rest with the Congregational prayer book in one hand and a dish of water in the other. It turned out well and the nurse returned the baby to the incubator and escorted me into the mother's room. She was asleep when we arrived, so the nurse awakened her and told her that her child had been baptized by Rev. Polk and pointed to me. There I stood and, as she cleared her eyes, she began to wail feverishly. I was not sure her crying was because I was Negro or because she had not had an update on the condition of her child. At any rate, she quieted down, smiled and the nurse told her how well the baptism went. The nurse also explained that I was a summer interim minister at the Congregational Church. The mother smiled and thanked me.

Rev. Hirons was a fine mentor/teacher and friend. He and his wife Dorothy and daughter Nancy were great to have me as house guests for the summer months and we broke bread together many a night. Plus, whenever they were invited out by parishioners, I was always included. In that way, I had a base to visit church members when necessary and interacted with the positive ones professionally and in friendship. All of this provided opportunities to get to know other town's people who were delighted at my presence.

This was the summer when the Federal Government had broken yet another treaty with the Affiliated Tribes at Ft. Berthold and rerouted the direction of the Missouri River to create what is called the Garrison Dam. In doing this, they relocated the Native Americans from their sacred and community capital, known as Elbowoods, which had been their gathering and living place for hundreds of years. The U.S. Government relocated them to an area, high up on a hill, and created a new town called New Town, ND. This was to be a mixed multi-racial community where the uprooted Native Americans would live, work and assemble for the future. This was not appreciated at all by the residents of Ft. Berthold who had fought for years to keep this from happening, but to no avail.

The big day took place that summer when I was there. President Dwight Eisenhower was to ride down the Missouri River on a barge, with his entourage, and dedicate the newly created Garrison Dam built by the Army Corps of Engineers.

I talked my teens, with the help of some fathers, into building a hotdog stand and to be on hand to sell hot dogs and Cokes to those on the sidelines waiting for a glimpse of the President. It was a bust. There were few folks on the banks of the river and not many hot dogs were sold – it was close to harvest time. Alas, such is life.

The final multi-cultural and somewhat exciting experience in what I thought would be a dull and anti-race summer, was serving a small town and its Congregational Church in Max, ND. Rev. Hirons took me there one day and laid out the responsibilities his church had for maintaining the Max church. This included tasks such as holding services once every six or eight weeks, keeping the weeds down, and caring for the upkeep of the church. When it was my turn, I took two of my Junior High students to do what was expected on the outside of the church. These were all ol' Russian people of Ukrainian background and when one gentleman saw us attempt-ing to use a scythe, he took us in hand and showed us how it was done—better than a lawnmower.

On the pastoral side, when Rev. Hirons and family left for vacation, I was in charge. All went smoothly. My preaching was modestly good (according to some). I made house calls and fulfilled other pastoral duties. Great kudos go to the young people who were generous, upbeat, funny, and cooperative in all we attempted that summer.

As things began to wind down, I realized what an enriched, meaningful and multi-cultural summer I had experienced, just the opposite from what I was anticipating due to the critical racial bias which seemed to grip parts of the church and community. I was ending on a Rocky Mountain High based upon my relationships with so many of church and town folk, plus the activities I managed to stumble into when least expected. That is truly one of the ways God has made himself known to me and motivated my life. To top it all off, two extraordinary things happened. When I preached my last Sunday, a few more people seemed to be in church than usual. I was not sure if it was in appreciation or the joy of seeing me leave. Nonetheless, when I was greeting people at the close of worship, a couple I had not recognized before were at the end of the line. They shook my hand and smiled and introduced themselves as the parents whose baby I baptized that anxious, hot morning at the hospital. The baby was cute and bouncy, and the parents expressed their sincere thanks. The husband worked with the Army Corps of Engineers that was building the Garrison Dam.

Secondly, I had worked out a plan to have Hazel's son, Wade and his best friend Bruce Hummel, to travel back to Chicago with me to meet my family, take in a ball game and play along the block where I had grown up and played as a kid, and meet some of my wonderful neighbors. That all worked out well and I sent them back on the CB&Q Empire Builder that would arrive in Minot at five the next morning and where they would be met by their parents. This was all a treat for the ways in which the boys helped me do some of the grungy chores around the church, work at the Max church and more.

Part II

"To all earth's creatures God has given the broad earth,
the springs, the rivers, and the forests, (giving) the air to the
birds, and the waters to those who live in water, (giving)
abundantly to all the basic needs of life, not as a private
possession, not restricted by law, not divided by boundaries,
but as common to all, amply and in rich measure."

- Gregory of Nazianzus

From: *Dakota* by Kathleen Norris

Congregational Church of Berthold, North Dakota

1955
Pastor of the Congregational Church of Berthold, ND

Rev. Treat and I had a good working relationship. He was pleased with my work in Garrison, as needed both by the church members and in the written report they submitted at the end of the summer. However, Rev. Treat must have been a glutton for punishment, for he pushed the race card one more time.

You see, the downside of being Black in a predominately White denomination is the scarcity of Black parishes wanting pastors, especially in major cities. The few churches we have in large cities were already staffed by elderly, venerable well-trained and seasoned Black pastors. There were few places for them to go within the denomination, so they remained in those churches until death or retirement. Some of our smaller Black churches were in the south and my mother was dead set against my going south because she had stumbled upon a failed lynching prior to coming to Chicago with her family. She had strong racial resentment against White people and did not mind saying so. However, when I entertained White friends at home, she was a marvelous and welcoming host, along with my father and other family members (my brothers were in the military service during these years).

Alas, upon graduating from seminary in the spring of 1955, I had not received "a call" to a church. So, there I was, a seminary graduate and without a "call".

I spent the summer in Clinical Pastoral Training at a notorious psychiatric hospital in New Jersey, along with five other clergy and a well-trained and supportive supervisor. Seminary students were urged to enroll in at least one quarter (three months), of Clinical training to help them round out their pastoral skills in parish ministry.

The hospital in New Jersey was called Greystone Park. It's census was large, and it was known as one of the most difficult mental hospitals in the state. It can best be described like the movie, "One Flew Over the Cuckoo's Nest." It created a great experience I have long valued throughout my min-istry in working with all sorts and conditions of mentally deranged people. There were times when we interacted with a certain group of patients who would remind us that the only difference between them and us, (the clergy team) was that we carried the keys. There was probably a great deal of truth in their judgement.

Still without a job, some of my classmates contacted Rev. Ed Treat, ex-plaining my desperate situation. Rev. Treat phoned me from North Dakota. Following a lengthy conversation regarding my aspirations and issues around locating a church, he pointedly asked, "If I am able to find a church in North Dakota that would call you, would you come?" After a brief hes-itation, I answered in the affirmative, thinking that would probably never happen, especially given Garrison Church's experience before I arrived.

Within a month, once again he pulled one out of the hat, informing me that he had a church willing for me to become their pastor on a two-year trial basis and that race was not an issue. The church was in the town of Berthold, ND. They had not had a full-time minister in fifteen years and would be willing to give it a try to see if a full-time person could help grow the church membership and move on from there. His only warning was about the salary, which was $2700 per year, plus parsonage and other ben-efits his office would pick up. Following my iron clad promise to Rev. Treat, I had no choice but to agree and accept the conditions offered – sight un-seen.

Excitement, hope, and redemption flooded my life as I followed through with ordination plans at my home church in Chicago and headed, once again, to the great state of North Dakota. As I allowed my mind to picture this new call and opportunity, I ended up comparing it to a blind date, since it was sight unseen. You take what you get and make the most of it, sometimes you score big and others, well, you simply endure. My life, as a Negro, has been bereft of options and I think that is true of most Black

Some of my Berthold teens

people in my age category. We seldom had many, if any, choices in life. Given the history of our struggle, many of us simply learned to accept what is offered and take it from there. I certainly was not a passive person but recognized over the years how few my options really were. I also attribute some of this from my wonderful father and the circumstances that surrounded his life and upbringing. Born to enslaved parents, of President James K. Polk linage, who wandered around for work in Reconstruction, with sixteen siblings and no stability in the process. He was finally given away to a Black medical doctor and his wife who brought him to Chicago for rearing, along with their son and he did the best he could to make it after marrying my mother. They had six children and father never slacked off when it came to his faith, church, wife, work and children. Without options, he simply had to accept what was handed to him without complaint. Despite all of this, he went about his life and work with a sense of quietness and confidence.

Sight unseen and without a personal interview, I had little in the way of expectations. I simply was eager to get out there and do what I had been taught and "called" to do. That was my initial reaction to Berthold. But, as you will discover, we grew together and it became an extraordinary experience. And for two years I pastored some of the finest, most hardworking, dedicated, and appreciative farming folk one could ever hope to meet and, at times, under some of the most daunting circumstances, especially the winters!

And so, once again, I boarded the CB&Q's great Empire Builder in Chicago's Union Station, heading for Minot, ND. Out at four in the afternoon and arriving at five the next morning. This allowed me much time to examine the meaning of my life and this call as to what it might portend for the future. Some of this reflection carried with it fear and trepidation, but that never lasted long.

When dinner was announced, I headed back to the diner and the steward gave me a window seat as I looked out observing the beauty of what was passing and what to expect. I had a fun waiter and got to know some of the others. I believe I was the last one to leave the dining car before it closed. By that time, the waiters all knew I had once been one of them, working for the same company. So we could chat and share jokes and stories. When it came to my destination, the steward and my waiter asked, "Why Minot?" Before I could answer, they went on to say how seldom it is for Black folk to get off in Minot. And, as one looked to the other, there was a nod, a wink and a smile on both faces. It was some months later that I discovered what that was all about and, yes, having to do with Third Street!

Upon arriving in Minot, I was met by Rev. Forrest B. Sharkey, pastor of the First Congregational Church of Minot. I later discovered he was a high-profile pastor of a sizable congregation with high visibility and involved in the wider community. He also served the Berthold church periodically when called upon.

Rev. Sharkey and I had become friends at a few church youth rallies, and conferences and weren't strangers. Once my trunk and baggage were unloaded, we headed for his home and spent the next couple of hours in his office talking about ND in general and Berthold, in particular. At breakfast time, I met his wife, two teenage children plus an exchange student from Turkey, who was to be with them for the school year. It was great meeting all of them and we had lots of fun at the breakfast table as I picked up bits and pieces about the family, Minot, school and more.

I rested and, that afternoon, we expected the Keiser family from Berthold to come, fetch me and drive me back to town. It all worked well. The Keiser family consisted of Fred, Sr., wife Edna and daughter Kay and son Freddy. Kay and Freddy were respectively in Senior High and Junior High school.

Fred, Sr. was one of the major farmers in the area. He was also chairman of the church's trustee board. His wife Edna was a Church School teacher, active in the women's society and involved in other aspects of the church. We hit it off well and they, over a short period, became my primary friends, parishioners, and confidants. With all the fine planning for my arrival and the joy of meeting the Sharkey family and the Keiser family, as we drove out to Berthold, I continued to have that burning question I refused to ask anyone prior to accepting this post. But as we neared the town, my question was answered. I saw no high-water tower which said BERTHOLD on it. And, therefore, my long, unstated assumption was correct. Berthold was a town without running water or indoor facilities!

We drove immediately to the American Legion Hall on Main Street. The Little Flock of my church had invited most of the town to a welcoming covered dish dinner for the new pastor of the Congregational Church, yours truly! It was at the peak of the harvest season and the farmers came to the dinner right out of the fields in their work clothes. The women were decked out in their lovely dresses with gingham aprons, hair stylish and all looked quite smart and lovely, keeping an eye on all that went in and out of the kitchen like a smorgasbord. It was here that I had my first taste of Scandinavian cuisine which I would soon learn to enjoy as it was often served in many homes.

The Keisers' made sure I met as many people as possible, especially those who were members of "Our" church. And of course, for me, the fun of the evening was watching the little tow-headed children peeking out behind their mother's aprons, looking at me, full of curiosity and awe. Adults deemed it politically incorrect to show signs of anything unusual on this history making occasion, even for the little hamlet of Berthold. They just rolled with the punches, I'd say, and were graceful. The older children and teens came off as complacent and held their ground. I would love to have been a fly on the walls in most homes that evening as the families discussed my presence as the new pastor in town and him being Black.

The Congregational Church and parsonage, on the same plot of land, were tidy and well-kept. The four-room white clapboard house sitting flat on the ground had a path leading out back to the biffy – as I had suspected. The house was freshly painted and adorned with durable furniture and dec-

Teenagers in the Berthold Church

orations, no doubt from the homes of the parishioners. The kitchen and refrigerator were filled with all kinds of homemade goodies for the new bachelor pastor, for which I was grateful. To top it all, there was no running water except a well. To get drinking water, a card was put in the window and water was delivered. You just had to hope that it lasted until the next delivery.

The house had three forms of heat: propane heater in the second bedroom, which became my study and office, oil burner in the living room which heated both the living room and the adjacent bedroom, plus the kitchen stove fired by propane and wood.

That first morning, after a good night's sleep and breakfast from an as-sortment of goodies provided by the church ladies, it was time to make that journey to the "path to the outhouse." I had put it off as long as pos-sible. I set off gingerly, knowing this was to become a regular trip. When I opened the door, lying there were 3-4 huge snakes, larger than the bulk of my arms, curled up comfortably. The snakes won!

I closed the door in dismay and called my mother in Chicago. She calmed me down and told me to go to Sears, since they have everything. I made it to the Keiser's for relief. Then I got it touch with Sears in Minot. Sure enough, they carried a portable water and chemical toilet that I ordered. I placed it in the closet of the second bedroom, which I used as a study, library and work place. I never saw those snakes again!

Some years later, reflecting on this experience, I realized that some of the town's jesters had played a prank on me. Later they removed the snakes.

The church, white clapboard, was small with seating capacity of about fifty, central pulpit, choir loft, and communion table and piano. The basement was used as a fellowship hall, Sunday School rooms and more. It also had a kitchen and coal and wood burning furnace.

The town was without paved streets, sidewalks, or streetlights. Main Street had the traditional stores and shops, three grocery stores, three taverns, John Deere and Case farm equipment stores, filling stations/auto shops, post office and Berthold Tribune newspaper office. A few decades earlier it could have looked like movie sets for the likes of Gun Smoke or High Noon. Homes and the three churches were scattered beyond Main Street. There was the Roman Catholic Church, red brick, as I recall, the Lutheran Church and my church on the same block. The house next to mine was the Lutheran parsonage. The Baptist church was a bit out of town. This is where the Negro from Chicago's South Side would live, realizing there were more people in the one square block there than in the entire town of Berthold.

If would be difficult for you to paint this picture or even try to imagine it. But let's give it a try:

IMAGINE, IF YOU CAN, a twenty-seven-year-old Negro, born and reared in the City of Chicago, with all the marginal comforts of his race and people, a college and seminary graduate, taking up residence in Berthold and under these somewhat, primitive circumstances with little frame of reference to survive such a life.

IMAGINE, IF YOU CAN, this Negro being told that he was the forty-eighth Negro in the entire state of North Dakota and would go from month to month without seeing another person of color, or especially Negro.

IMAGINE, IF YOU CAN, having to learn the culture and mores of predominantly Nordic community of farmers and small-town folk, in some way, still tethered to their homelands and who were without urban, not to mention interracial or multicultural sophistication.

IMAGINE, IF YOU CAN, living among such people not knowing if either your presence or the gospel of Jesus Christ or the concept of brotherhood and that all people are equal could reach them, and not knowing – racially speaking – whether they were friend or foe.

IMAGINE, IF YOU CAN, living in a town in which the only telephone was connected to the central operator. You had to call her and she would connect you with the outside line. Of course, she listened to most calls and knew everyone's business. It was of those oak wall phones with a crank dial to the central operator.

IMAGINE, IF YOU CAN, this six-foot, stocky Black man trying to navigate his first Saturday night bath in the big, galvanized tub on the back porch. I cleaned the tub, put a kettle of water on the stove and, when it was boiling hot, I poured it into the tub. It amounted to one inch of water. I pulled the shades, dipped my big toe in, and the water was already getting cold.

But I had to take that leap of faith and do what had to be done. I tried to wash from the top down, but that too did not work very well. The water kept getting colder and colder. Finally, I completed the job in ice cold water. Try to imagine this!

A few days later, I told my story of woe to Fred and Edna Keiser. They decided on a routine that saved my life and ministry there. The Keiser's had a cistern in their basement with water used to supply the entire house, in-door bathroom and all. The plan was, I would come to their home on Sat-urday nights for dinner, a shower, and to watch Lawrence Welk on TV (there were not many TV's in town) and then I returned home to tidy up my sermon, bank the furnace fire at the church and get ready for Sunday morning.

Later, I discovered, in going to visit parishioners at the hospital in Minot, that there was a brand-new YMCA in the center of the city. It had all of the facilities one could ask for like a swimming pool, a steam bath— and showers! So, I made more trips to visit patients in the Minot hospital than you can imagine. And I became squeaky clean. Once again, I never realized that one day the Minot YMCA would provide my next vocational step.

The story I am telling is doubtless not one that many other Negroes, at that time, had ever experienced. This instance and more came into play as I settled in and made my home and carried out my pastoral vocation and responsibilities under such circumstances.

In retrospect, this was truly a groundbreaking milestone. A rural lily-white church out on the northern most state of the Great Plains hiring a Negro pastor from the City of Chicago. Though small and insignificant by today's standards, this social and racial arrangement was four or five decades ahead of its time. White churches simply did not hire Negro pastors, not even the most "liberal." Furthermore, recalling Dr. King's adage, that eleven o'clock on Sunday morning is the most segregated hour in America since they do not even worship together.

There was a lot of "getting to know you" in this somewhat dynamic and fluid situation. Close your eyes and put yourself in either position and notice the stark contrasts: Given our extraordinarily diverse backgrounds, we were both willing to take this risk of getting to know each other in most unusual ways: racial, political, social, economic, work, educational and theological. What contrasts! In all of this, we found the middle way, learned to respect, appreciate, and honor each other's lifestyles and found that the gospel of Jesus Christ was the binding cord that united us.

With all these differences, the one thing I had going for me was that I was no stranger to being among, knowing or working with White people. So often in seminars, speeches, and workshops, in later years, I emphasize how much more Black people know about White people than vice versa. Along with that idea, I made sure White people knew that Black people are not a monolithic group. These cardinal issues of race 101 are critical for a more mature understanding when it comes to race relations or anti-racism training or discussions. I was ahead of the game when it came to feeling comfortable in this new situation where I never saw another person who looked like me for months. This was not true for them as they caught glimpses of me on the streets, in the shops, cafe and visiting parishioners.

My mentor, pastor, and friend, Rev. Sharkey, known as "Pops" Sharkey, managed for me to buy a used car within a month of my arrival. It was an old gray Ambassador Nash, standard drive and bulky as can be imagined, but it got me around to visit church members, most of whom were working large sections of land as their farms, not acres but sections (640 acres of land equals one section).

The land was extremely flat, and one could see for miles with nothing to interfere with one's vision. The land was so flat, I could drive, fall asleep from the monotony of the terrain and roads, wake up eight to ten miles later and never leave the road or go into the ditch. Or as one friend here in the church I attend in Philadelphia, who spent his teen years in ND put it, "We used to say, the land was so flat, you could see for three days looking straight ahead." And as for the soil, it lacked sand and was all hard turf, thus it would stick to your boots and shoes. It was difficult to plow or cultivate and created clogs of mud when wet.

A pastor in such a rural village had to be multi-talented: conduct worship and preach, direct the choir, teach Sunday school, do some snow shoveling when the winter set in and no one else was nearby, bank the fire in the furnace on Saturday nights for a warm, toasty church service Sunday morning, as well as do secretarial work and care for the parsonage. It was a great way to break into the real life of a pastor for later years and I developed empathy for all the tasks needed to be undertaken by staff or volunteers.

When it came to preaching, I tossed away the old sermons and simply could not recall what I had to say on most Sunday mornings. Again, I stuck to the middle of the ground on whatever the text or issues fleshed out. My most conservative parishioners did not mind taking issue when our theology clashed, but they were most often gracious and understanding following the discussion.

As for racism in Berthold, for the most part it was more implicit than explicit. A few grumpy old men expressed their feelings and attitudes to their wives and children about my being a Negro called to be the church's pastor. From all indications, they never attended church anyway, except for funerals and weddings or when their children were baptized. But the feedback was there. And there was the time, on a cold winter's evening, when the talk at one of one of the three town taverns included going over to the parsonage and giving the N... a scare. Cooler heads prevailed and it never happened. Some in the bar, who were getting to know me, spoke out against such talk and it died down.

Several times I asked Fred and Edna Keiser, who were among my closest friends, about the church's conversation calling me and how much race did play into the discussion. They were always clear and said, that was never an issue. Even years later, when visiting the Keiser's in Arizona, over dinner one evening, I returned to the question of my race in calling me to Berthold, and again, they reiterated, the color of your skin was not an impediment. Fortunately, Fred and Edna were not only leading laypersons in my congregation, but also in the town, and they farmed numerous sections of land. They were highly respected.

My arrival in Berthold in 1955 coincided with the brutal lynching/slaughtering of Emmett Till. My burden was heavy, and I was in despair. There was no one with whom I could discuss and share my deep sorrow. I recall having to carry that anger and sadness deep within. The murder gained little traction in the Minot Daily News and few words in the Berthold Tribune. All of which made it difficult to me to suppress that event and other atrocities against Negroes that followed. Till lived in my neighborhood and attended the same elementary school my siblings and I attended decades earlier. Our parents helped rear a foster daughter who was a classmate of Emmett Till. I grieved silently and via mail to family and friends. It must have been that kind of thing my mother feared for me, had I taken a parish in the south.

I compared this experience to what missionaries must have felt going out into the world of other nations, cultures, and people to do whatever their mission and passion demanded. They lived and raised their families in unusual racial and cultural circumstances, and many took on the life and culture of the indigenous people with whom they worked. Thus, this was the image I conjured up periodically as to why am I here?

Other than breaking bread and feasting at the farms of parishioners as well as my in-town parishioners, I managed to host fellow Congregational North Dakota clergy passing through town, became a fan and follower of the Berthold high school basketball team, and learned to play bid-whist, ice fish, and suffer the extreme, severe, long dark days and sub-zero temperatures that too often defined North Dakota. The coldest I experienced was minus thirty-eight degrees. Snow would fall on top of snow. Days later, fierce winds would pick it up and it seemed as if it was snowing all over again with snowbanks between six and eight feet high. This required hand shoveling, long before the invention of snow-blowers.

Two college students from Minot read about me in the Minot Daily

News and ventured out to Berthold for dialogue and dinner periodically. They both had leanings towards the ministry and wanted to discuss my life, education, when I felt "the call," race relations, politics and more. We became close friends and I looked forward to these gatherings. They were Gene Afseth and David Waldron. In turn, they introduced me to Minot, its history and some of its critical social issues. Background information and the history of "Third Street" often surged to the top of our talks to the extent they decided the three of us should take a "field trip" and check out this well-known but seldom talked about institution in the Magic City. And we did!

Of course, my parishioners would have thrown the Book at me had they known of these plans. Afseth and Waldron filled me in on the fact that there was a substantial Red -Light District, with an engrained history in Minot, unlike any other city in ND. I was told that the majority of the Ladies of the Night happened to be Negroes. This fact certainly sparked my interest in pastoral and sociological concern, as there were no other Black men around (except those owners who supported the institution).

We ventured forth. Most of the sporting houses were fronted by signs reading Bar-B-Q, Café, juke joints and more.

The field trip was on. We decided to have dinner at one of the Bar-B-Q cafes. The owner/manager was a Black male, professional, warm, and friendly. He was somewhat taken aback seeing me but did not let on. Perhaps he thought these were two new White clients (Johns) with a Black newcomer to the area.

As I recall, a couple of ladies peered out from behind curtains and smiled. It did not take long before they decided we either did not know what was going on or didn't have the know-how to take the initiative. OR, that we might be undercover cops casing the joint. Whatever, the meal was fine, and we paid our bill, left tips, and hastened out.

It was the Third Street story that gave me a clue as to what the dining car steward and the waiter meant when asking me why I was going to Minot. With a wink and a nod, I now understood their body language and interest. That was our one and only visit, but Third Street often became a catch phrase, especially when I moved from Berthold to Minot. There's a great deal more about this phenomenon described during the period when

I worked in Minot. This was the hot-button topic that called out race and racism.

The Congregational Church of Berthold did their best to grow the numbers and return the church to where it could support a pastor and ministry, but it just was not in the cards. There was little growth in the town and those who were church people were already committed to either the Catholic Church, the Baptist, or the Lutheran Church. The unchurched often found their way to the Congregational church for Christmas, Easter, baptisms, and funerals. But there was no commitment otherwise. My color seemed not to have made a difference once they got over the initial shock. I was genuinely received and moved about without the thought of being different, except when I saw myself in the mirror each morning.

Up to this point I believe I had adjusted well into my first parish. The little flock was becoming comfortable with me, home and hospital visits went well, and, even with the intense weather, I tried my best to adjust and take it in stride.

However, the unexpected came when we reached Advent and Christmas. But here again, I managed to do all the proper things for the season, a few new ol' timers from town managed to find their way to the Congregational Church and all was cozy.

On Christmas Eve, friends and members dropped off gifts and wonderful canned food at the parsonage, while I was at church making final preparation for the Christmas Eve service. All went well and the church was beautiful and full.

Upon returning home to the many gifts and goodies, I became anxiously aware that no one had extended an invitation for me to share Christmas Eve or Christmas Day. Eight or ten weeks prior to Christmas, I had ordered and received a fine black and tan German shepherd puppy. Biff was cute, rambunctious, and high spirited. So, there we were, just the two of us alone throughout the day. This was the very first time, before or since, that I have been alone on this great festive day.

It was so cold in the lower extremities of the house; I could see Biff's breath whenever he barked. And this made me conscious of how cold it was for me from the knees down to the floor. Had the men placed the sod around the house, this would have been avoided.

One of the Juke Joints on 3rd St., Minot

I had breakfast with Biff, listening to Harry Belafonte sing Christmas carols in his calypso accent along with a couple of other Christmas albums. This was what constituted that special day — and I was alone!

When I finally connected with the central operator in Berthold and had her call my family in Chicago, I was almost in tears. Hearing my parents' voices and the others at home in the background really got to me. Everything was fine, but I just could not understand why I had not been invited to be with one of the church families.

A few days later, as I ran into church members and they inquired about my Christmas, I was perfectly candid by indicating I was all alone the entire day. The upshot of it was that, as the parishioners began chatting with one another the following Sunday, they realized the great social error. Each had thought the other had invited me over for Christmas and, as a result, no one invited me to share in the day. So much for assumptions!

From that Christmas forward, and given that unforgettable experience, I pledged to myself that I would always seek out folk whom I thought were alone during major holidays and invite them to share with me, my family, and others. And so it has been for the remainder of my years.

I learned, early on, just how difficult it was to read the minds and thoughts of Scandinavians. They were somewhat stoic, and their joys and sorrows seemed to have no boundaries. The great Danish psychiatrist, Soren Kierkegaard, used the term "melancholy" in describing his Scandi-

Dee D. Govan Grill on 3rd St.

navian heritage and I could understand this sentiment. This has borne itself out, from my observations, over the years.

From all indications, there was genuine esteem and appreciation for my ministry there. However, there was no overblown reaction when they knew, as did I, that the two-year experiment would soon end.

I had great respect and appreciation for my little flock and the people of Berthold, most of whom had been considerate, kind, generous and gracious, when it came to me, my work and presence there.

It did not take me long to realize my urban and debonair comfort zone had been upended. I had to reimagine much of my entire life, culture, and history to adapt to this new normal, which was undoubtedly rural. The land and all that that meant so much to these agrarian people, came from the fact that most of them had left their countries to come to this part of America for a new start. They cherished the good earth, giving and withholding regardless of their dependency upon it. The way of life for these people, who were wedded to it, was astonishing. They had deep faith in God, the Scriptures and an abiding trust, even when things did not work out as expected. It took a while for this city slicker to catch up with all of this and what it portended to those whose lives were invested in rural North Dakota.

I was allowed to try any and everything I needed to know about farm life from milking cows and picking up rocks. None of which came easy and

Learning the ABCs of farming 1955

I did not rank in the upper echelons in the grading system. But I managed. When everything worked out from planting season, with adequate rain and moisture to harvest, that constituted a very good year. They were not all that way. Whenever I now sing the harvest hymn, Come Ye Thankful People Come, it resonates more deeply with me and carries more weight and understanding than on the years before my Dakota days. These ol' pioneers were deeply dedicated to the land, their vocation and, to use the title of one of my favorite books about that part of the country in its early days, they were, to paraphrase, giants in the earth.

The farewell events went smoothly and were heartfelt. I would second those who say how easy it is to fall in love with one's first parish, for a host of reasons! And so, it was with Berthold. I had fought the good fight with all the help possible from my little flock, and Rev. Ed Treat. Now it was time to move on.

But before going on to the next phase of my ministry in ND, let me talk about the weather that required extreme attention, as well as providing re-markable experiences.

AND WHAT ABOUT THE CLIMATE?

What can anyone say about the unrelenting winters in North Dakota? I thought a Windy City, Chicago boy, had seen and felt it all when it came to bad weather. A person must live in that state to know and understand the true meaning of winter! Furthermore, exactly what happens and what do people do during that time of year?

Here are a few stories from several farmers, from their olden days of horse, buggy and sleigh, plus my firsthand accounts—what I witnessed, experienced and endured. My beloved old friends back home, even jug-buddies, cannot wrap their heads around how I managed to cope with all of this.

To set the stage, these were the days before our homes and workplaces were saturated with radios, and there was almost no TV. There were no weather forecasters and the Farmers' Almanac was the mainstay.

My little four room house, minus indoor plumbing, had not been completely fortified for the winter! The men were working during harvest when I arrived and had precious little time to bank around the house with sod to keep the biting wintery winds from bellowing into the house from the floors upwards. Regardless of the heating systems, the lower part of the house was always drafty and cold. Or, in my case, from the knees down, it was frigid and whenever my puppy Biff barked, you could see his breath.

To start with the extreme temperatures and long before the wind chill factor, I experienced minus 38 degrees! (Hold that point):

•Nostrils would freeze; eyelids felt as though they would freeze and not open with each blink; hands, fingers, feet, and more were bitterly cold and off the charts, if you were not prepared for such temperatures – and I wasn't, in the beginning.

•All automobiles had to have head bolt heaters to plug into the electric circuit near their homes to keep the radiators in their cars from freezing. Every car was recommended to have an emergency survivors kit containing a blanket, candle, health bars, water and so forth, especially for distance and, especially, night driving in the state. In those sub-zero temperatures, if one runs into a ditch and can't drive out, he/she will not die from the cold, but the thin air is likely to put one to sleep (hypoxemia occurs) and then death comes from the coldness.

• The days are short and there are long periods of darkness. At the peak of winter, the darkness starts about between four to five in the evenings and the sun does not rise before eight in the mornings. Of course, things shifted dramatically in warmer weather. From mid-June to September there were 16 hours of daylight and the temperature can reach to 100 hundred in the middle of summer (which, I was told, is similar to Scandinavia weather and climate).

• There were winter hobbies and other ways to keep sane from so much darkness, especially in these pre-TV, electricity and what we call modern conveniences. Many men ice fished. They build ice houses and when the ice reaches the depth of 12 to 14 inches, they drive their pick-ups on the ice and set up their ice houses — some quite elegant and fancy, equipped with Coleman stoves/heaters, card tables and chairs. They usually drill four holes in each corner of the house to drop their lines for fish. They play bid whist, poker, and other card games, accompanied by lots of liquid nourishment to keep the body warm (ha!).

• Women, of course, tend the house and with children or neighbors or church groups, knit, make quilts, tat, cook, sew, and help with the farm chores. I've been told that in the old days, the snow would be so high in drifts that farmers would string a line between the house and the barn and use it to hold onto when slushing from house to barn in the dark and vice versa.

• Of course, other winter activities, back in the day, would include hunting, trapping animals for pelts to be sold to the furriers in town (when fur coats were in vogue like fox, mink, raccoon and more).

• Finally, let me mention how the weather happens and can change so rapidly. The best example: a snowstorm can blow in and leave between six inches to a foot of fluffy dry snow all over the place. Temps can be zero to in the single digits. Over the next couple of days, the sun will come out, and all will be beautiful and calm. Then along will come a fierce wind that picks up the already fallen snow and turns that same snow into a blizzard that upends everything. That same snow will be tossed around and end up as snowbanks as high as six feet or more. Temps will fall way below zero and last a few days. Suddenly, the chinook winds blow in from Montana or Canada and send the temperature up twenty degrees. You will come to think you have died and gone to heaven and feel how warm it is @ ten above zero!

• Before the automobile, the stories are often reported of how farmers would go into town on their horse-drawn sleds, spend a few hours shopping, and so forth, and along would come a chinook wind, melting the ice and snow to the extent the farmer could not return home because there was no more snow.

I recall two luncheon meetings where the speakers called for a name change for "North" Dakota. The thesis was it was difficult to attract business and people due to the bad rap ND had about its weather.

Learning to drive/navigate in ND sub-zero weather of snow-banks and unplowed streets was a real art. A couple of my parishioners made sure I learned these skills, after bailing me out of a few untenable situations. Their instructions have served me well for the years that have followed.

So much for the weather!

Now let me tell you about the most remarkable and life-changing event from my time there.

It was the night I had my "come to Jesus moment."

It was a cold winter's evening. The temperature was hovering down in the low single digits, I believe. Before turning in, I noticed a light burning in the church. So, I bundled up to go over and turn it out.

When I opened my kitchen door, leading to the church, I was overwhelmed by the sky and almost fell on my knees. It was daunting as well as awesome! At a second look, I realized I was experiencing what my sixth-grade science teacher had tried to explain to my class of urban, Negro kids in Chicago. It was something he said we probably would never see called the Northern Lights or The Aurora Borealis. There it was in all its grace, beauty and splendor. It was so beautifully dominating and was like dancing through the glorious, splendid sky.

I quickly pulled a chair from the kitchen, along with my trusty Hudson Bay blanket, and simply sat and watched in dead silence for over an hour. That was, for me, the firmament on high, the likes of which I had never witnessed before or since.

My mind worked overtime as I sat and watched.

I was flooded with thoughts from Genesis, several of the Psalms, espe-cially Ps. 19:1 "The heavens are telling the glory of God; and the firmament proclaims his handiwork." And indeed, it did! This led to James Weldon Johnson's iconic poem, Creation, which all Black children had to learn by heart and recite in Sunday School or at public school assemblies: "And God stepped out on space..." There came to mind the number of times I listened to or sang in choral groups, Haydn's great oratorio "The Creation." My thoughts even took me back to my days in my church youth fellowship on Sunday evenings, when, if we were lucky, there would be a sing-along of our favorite hymns, played by our most gifted pianist and teenage member of the group, Angela Batteast. When it was my turn, I belted out hymn number 144 noted for both its words and walking bass parts. The hymn writer not only drew upon Psalm 19 and others depicting God's great cre-ation of heaven and earth, but, in my way of thinking, he too must have witnessed the Northern Lights before composing the hymn, "The Spacious Firmament on High."

My preaching and faith greatly improved after that experience. God was in his heavens, and all was right with the world, so the saying goes… And I was convinced!

Before leaving my remembrances of Berthold, let me highlight another significant parishioner I knew there.

Walter Troxel was a strong leader in the community as reflected by his love of family, church, social commitment, and all to the glory of God! He had been a Republican State Senator, having served in that capacity for many years, and he was highly respected throughout the state. Though a deeply religious, almost fundamentalist leaning churchman, he was well noted for being an arch conservative in most aspects of his life. In all of these and, despite all of this, Walter was a devoted member of my church—no doubt the most liberal church in the Berthold community, both theologically and socially.

You can imagine this distinguished gentleman, moving past his mid-eighties, sitting in church every Sunday listening to my liberal brand of theology, with pinches of liberal political and social justice thrown in. When he was at odds with something I said, and that was often, he never failed to call my attention to it following morning worship. Though he could be a strong critic, once we had an opportunity for dialogue, he could give that infectious twinkle of a smile, shake my hand, and walk away shaking his head. He was never angry or verbose, but in strong disagreement. As was often the case, we could disagree but never be disagreeable.

He and his wife, Mary, were wonderful parishioners and were given to hospitality, gracious in sharing their home and family farm of which he was both humble and proud.

One day he paid a surprise visit to me at the parsonage. The purpose of his call was that he had arranged for me, without my knowledge, to offer the invocation at the opening of the State Legislature, to which I agreed. Once again, a fly in the buttermilk!

The day arrived and Walter picked me up and we headed for Bismarck. He was proud to have this happen, knowing it would be a "first" for me and for the State Legislature. Upon arrival, he introduced me to his cronies and friends on the right side of the aisle, I think, and, at the appropriate time, he proudly escorted me to the podium, introduced me as his pastor and remained next to me as I prayed. Following the prayer, we returned to our seats and observed closely the business on the docket.

We had a cheerful chat upon returning to Berthold, as he explained some of the ins and outs of the legislative body for North Dakota. We steered clear of any contentious political, Biblical, or social issues. My thoughts reinforced my long-standing opinion of Walter Troxel. This was a great man, and it was no wonder why he was so highly adored and respected in all walks of life in the state, church and community. Where are the Walter Troxels of our day?

On that note, let's move forward.

As I began dusting off my resume and thinking about my future, I had an urgent call from Pops Sharkey of Minot. He needed to have a meeting with me and Mr. Ev Miller, Executive Secretary of the Minot YMCA. I agreed and we set a date and time.

The meeting was somewhat of a secret, but cordial, warm and friendly. They wanted me to know that I was needed in Minot and, if a job opened, for example, in the YMCA working with the teenagers, would I take it? They went on to make their case and explained it in more detail. All of which had to do with the US Air Force building an Air Base in Minot that would bring in over fifteen thousand airmen and their families. And, they said, of course many of the airmen would be persons of color. Added to this, and the fact that Minot had a poor or, better yet, no substantial record of working with or exposure to especially Negroes, it was their judgement that someone like me could be helpful to the community in helping to build that bridge with the military population and the civilian community.

As the base was under early construction, several its airmen had already come to town and were living in the Y's dormitories. With this group of early arrivals were troops of color, especially Negroes. They were generally accepted in town, but the town had not gotten used to them at this early point and signs of separation and segregation were beginning to surface, according to some of the Y residents who spoke with Mr. Miller and Mrs. Sharkey. Mrs. Sharkey was the office manager at the Y and responsible for renting out dormitory rooms.

Miller and Sharkey seemed to have had an epiphany. They saw the long-range implications and felt they had to develop a plan to mitigate against a strong anti-Negro situation before it became a major problem. In other words, they had the social insight that the leadership of the community or the Air Base had not recognized, at that point of the base's development (at least not publicly to my knowledge).

Their plan was to ask me to accept the Y job as Youth Program Secretary and use my presence and influence on issues of race to expose and help educate the population of Minot for a better attitude of tolerance towards race. The question was, would I accept it?

The Y youth director had recently resigned to take a new post in South Dakota. Mr. Miller, the Executive Secretary of the Y had not yet filled that position. It would mean working with close to four hundred Junior and Senior High School students through their club programs and other aspects of their relationships to the Y. That would be the paid job. The other piece of social responsibility concerned racial understanding and, what we might call today, helping to educate the community in multiculturalism. That would be accomplished through speeches, work at the Y with teens and other opportunities to educate the community about Negroes and other persons of color. As well, it was their desire for equity and equality in this new community and environment of Minot, North Dakota. Opportunities would be made available for me to speak, preach, and make myself available to organizations, churches and more in the community for this purpose.

In this 99.9% White community, their only frame of reference, when it came to Negroes, was Third Street where the women of the night were predominantly Negro and all that that portended for better racial understanding.

This challenging, duel responsibility fit well into my passion and portfolio. This was my strength, dating back to when I was a social activist growing up in Chicago. After a great deal of conversation with these two men and learning of their plan, I readily accepted the offer and the challenge.

Their next task was to take their proposal before the YMCA Board of Directors and, hopefully, get their approval on the spot and then announce my appointment before it leaked out into the wider community.

Their strategy was somewhat air-tight and their case was wholly relevant. It had never been thought about by other leaders in the community on that level or the possibility of my availability. Miller was able to pull out an affirmative commitment from his Board at that meeting. The editor and owner of the Minot Daily News was a Y Board member and the announcement of my appointment was a jaw-dropping story in the Minot Daily News the next morning. This was somewhat of a coup, if you will, on behalf of the Y Board, whose members were the shakers and movers of the Minot community.

The news story would carry most of the following details about me and my job.

"Rev. Robert L. Polk, current pastor of the Congregational Church of Berthold, ND, was called to be the new Youth Program Secretary of the Minot YMCA. Polk, a native of Chicago, completed his college degree from Doane College in Nebraska and his theological education from the Hartford Seminary of Connecticut. Rev. Polk will be the first Negro professional serving in the city of Minot and will bring healing, reconciliation, and wider racial understanding here, especially as the increasing population of the Air Base will enhance Minot in becoming a multi-racial and multi-cultural community, far greater than it has been.

Polk has had significant experience working with teenagers from all walks of life and will be a perfect fit for our Y young people."

Before the news hit the families and homes of Minoters, it was a done deal.

I would love to have been a fly on the wall as the staid ol' gentlemen of the Y Board dissected and hammered out the efficacy of such a hire.

Part III

"And when my time is up?
Have I done enough?
Will they tell my story?"

- *Hamilton* by Lin-Manuel Miranda

Minot, North Dakota
1957-1960

My first day and the subsequent week on the job was remarkable and unforgettable. The morning paper carried the article of my appointment and caught the city by surprise.

At around eleven-thirty, the first Junior High students were released for lunch. They almost mobbed the Y lobby and grill expecting to see, greet and shake hands with me. My keen, perceptive boss, Ev Miller, was prepared. He and I stood outside of the reception desk as the kids poured in. They seemed to be beyond themselves regarding my appointment. With smiles, disbelief, awe and more they passed by and had to greet Mr. Miller before they got to me, smiled, shook my hand and headed to the Y grill for lunch.There was a buzz throughout the building.

The second wave of students, the Senior High group, followed shortly thereafter and, more rambunctiously, made their way into the front lobby. Ev again was next to me, and they had to greet or deal with him before seeing and meeting me. There were smiles, warm handshakes, a couple of words and so it went. Once I passed muster in that routine, the students began to settle in and visit in my office or meet me in their clubs, the Grill and so forth. There was never a sense of scorn, bigotry, nor a racist attitude. That great song from The King and I reflected those early days: "Getting to know you." In all, we are talking about three hundred plus teenagers!

I can attest, as sociologists and others have said, and I have witnessed, that racial prejudice is lower among young people in our society. The several times it raised its ugly head will be spelled out in the pages that follow.

I discovered that the YMCA (and the Y) as a national and international organization was exciting and fascinating. Everett Miller was what I would

The YMCA in Minot

call a teaching boss, full of ideas, willing to share his wisdom, known for his empathy and compassion and, yet, a strong no-nonsense person. He was one of the finest bosses I have encountered: committed to the principles and values of the YMCA. It was easy to see the "Y" was his first love. He had come to Minot from the Minneapo6lis Y, endeared himself to the community, his board of directors and the many service clubs and Y's-Mens clubs. This was especially noticeable in that his predecessor, Colin Brown, years earlier, initiated the Y concept for Minot, the leaders bought into it and felt it was what the town's young people needed. Mr. Brown pulled together the town's fathers, and raised the money for such a fine building in downtown Minot, close to one of the Junior High Schools and the only high school. That was ideal and it thrived at the heart of youth endeavors in Minot. Unfortunately, a few years into his tenure, Mr. Brown died of a heart attack and Ev Miller was his successor.

Ev Miller filled Mr. Brown's shoes well and, after a few months, Miller had fit into this job and continued as the well-regarded new Minot YMCA Executive Director.

His wife, Dorothy, and two pre-teen children, Vicky and David, were key to his family life and they often invited me over for meals and R&R.

As a strong Methodist layman and dedicated Christian, one of Ev's priorities – somewhat subliminal – was to restore the "C" to the YMCA and now that he had a clergyman on his team as his Youth Program Secretary (youth director) he felt assured he could move in that direction. Miller also made it possible for me to attend weekend Y training sessions, workshops on Y history and philosophy and more. He was preparing me as a possible long term Y staffer. All of which indicated his respect for me and my work with the young people under my supervision.

Speaking about race, when the word hit the community about my hire, there were mixed feelings in homes and businesses. Little, if any, filtered in my direction, except for some of my teens who often shared the outrage expressed by their parents. "Having a Negro supervise and work with their children" as the face of the YMCA – more about this later, I'm sure that Ev Miller received his share of insults and jabs regarding my coming on board.

The Y was well equipped with a gym/fitness center, dormitory, swimming pool. This was the main attraction, with a full-time physical education director – my counterpart, Don Anderson, a very fine co-worker and colleague. Families, businessmen and younger children all had a place and found their niche at the Minot YMCA.

Years later, even today, sixty years later, whenever I think of the teenagers, back in my Y days, it brings joy to my heart and a smile to my face. They all brought gifts that differed. Like all young people of that era, they could be rebellious, petulant, disorderly and, at the same time, respectful, generous, caring, kind, loving, ever loyal and ready to be of service to others. Into this great mix, our goal was to nurture, advise, listen…and lead by example. And, by the grace of God and many tries and failures, I can say we crafted a program that ultimately was creative, innovative, and supportive of our young people.

My role as Youth Program Secretary was to help harness all that energy in our teens and help develop them further into good, caring young men and women as a part of their transition into adulthood. We, my team of advisors and staff, in a sense, were that fragile but important link between home and family, school, religious affiliation and the adult world in which they would soon be members. In short, throughout our clubs and activities, our role was to help nurture those young people in our care, in body, mind and spirit (the triangle logo of the YMCA worldwide). We were a part of that great social and spiritual movement in Minot, North Dakota. Or, as one student commencement speaker so richly said recently, (and I can say for our Y program), we gave our youth "roots to grow and wings to fly." And by all accounts, and as I have continued to be in touch with former Y students down through the decades, as well as several former advisors, this is the way most would describe their experience.

With the help of adult volunteers and programs selected by the youth in their Hi-Y and Tri-Hi-Y, Junior Hi-Y programs, we attempted to fulfill that responsibility and more.

My role was to make sure every club had one adult advisor. I recruited, trained, educated, and informed the leaders/advisors about what the Y hoped to instill into the lives of these young people: values, norms, civic and social responsibility, issues of citizenship, community service and Christian or spiritual values. The other two ethnic/religious' groups in the community were Greek and Jewish, all members and active at the Y.

This was the sum of our diversity, with the exception of one male Native American and several Asians, plus a few students whose skin tone indicated a mixed marriage along the way.

I realized that my work in race relations was cut out for me. My second responsibility, in accepting the job, was enabling youth, community leaders, families, churches and clubs to have conversation 101 in Negro history and race relations and help improve the atmosphere in this issue for the incoming men, women and families of color when they arrived at the Minot airbase that was under construction at the time of my hiring. It was a great opportunity and a daunting responsibility, and I worked assiduously at both. There was no basic frame of reference for most of the residents and little explicit racism, on balance. Much of what was there came from World War II vets and some of their experiences with Black troops and the ever-present hypocritical conversations about Third Street.

Here are a few of the overt instances of racism and anti-Negro issues etched enough in my memory for me to recall.

I would be remiss if I did not say that the giant elephant in the room, always, was the red-light district known in coded language as "Third Street", in which many, if not most of the ladies of the night, were Negroes, my soulmates. And, in practically every conversation I had or speech I gave regarding race, that was the issue that surfaced. In such dialogues, it was implied that "if it were not for Third Street, our community would be open and affirming and welcoming of the Air Force troops of color." The premise was that the city could warmly welcome airmen of color and their families since the racial animus or prejudice were due to all that Third Street represented and the blight it brings to the town. I always was dubious about that, even if the comments were not articulated. I often boldly asserted, "If it were not for your sons, husbands, neighbors and, in general, the White male population, Third Street could not exist." The Junior Chamber of Commerce report notes that Minot is the only city in North Dakota where there is such a deeply entrenched, sustained, historic area of prostitution. There are not such other clusters of prostitution across the state, even where there are other military installations. I rest my case and call for a deeper conversation regarding beliefs, prejudicial attitudes and misinformation about Negroes and other people of color. I can't be who I am without recognizing the role race played in my tenure in North Dakota as the forty-eighth official Negro resident of the state.

Let me be clear. Grace is implicit in the title of this narrative and my history there is personal. I will share some of the moments where I confronted both implicit and explicit racism, and how that could've inflicted harm on me and how I managed to deal with them, with no one to talk with to share this burden. First the incidents and, further, the coping skills I learned from my Black family roots, neighbors and church.

To start, before the days of widespread TV, computers, and other high technology, seeing a movie once a week, was a treat. The one prominent Negro actor that caught many peoples' eyes was Sidney Poitier. When I arrived, some identified me with Mr. Poitier and even said we looked alike – what a compliment! In their manner of thinking, all Negroes looked alike. Poitier became a hit and was, again, one of their positive early exposures to Negro people.

On another occasion, when my sister and brother-in-law visited me in Minot, my sister decided to go up to Main Street to window shop. She recalled two White men passing her and saying, "Looks like we have a new one in town."

I never heard a disparaging word to my face. But the father of one family, with a daughter about to be married, refused to have me officiate at her wedding. Rev. Sharkey substituted on my behalf and it was a seamless event.

There was more overt racism against Native Americans in and throughout North Dakota. We had one or two Native Americans in our programs, and they got along well. But not nearly enough considering the large Native American population in the city and nearby Ft. Berthold. The joke, for me, was the overt animosity between Norwegians and Swedes.

There were, of course, conversations about race in and about the city relating to my presence, the incoming of the airbase, among World War II veterans, as I mentioned before, and perhaps around the tables in many homes. But during my first two years there, none of this reached my ears— except the big one which deserves to be noted.

It was customary for me to close the Y for the weekend. The usual drill was to have one of the college student workers close the gym, swimming pool area, hit the lights. We then would head across the street to the Clarence Parker Hotel for a night-cap to top off the evening.

On that evening, the hotel lobby was full of guests attending a convention. We worked our way up to the bar, found two stools and waited to place our orders. The bartender continued to ignore us and, finally the student with me knew the bartender, also a Minot State Teachers College student, and they played football together. In what was too long a waiting period to be served, my student went back and reminded the bartender he had ignored us. The bartender replied that the manager of the hotel had sent out a notice not to serve Negroes anymore. Many Black airmen had already come into town and were not welcomed in some establishments. My student staff member explained to the bartender who I was and this new ruling in the hotel was not known in the community. The bartender relented and finally took my order. It was my first such experience. But the story does not end here.

I knew the manager of the hotel. We were both members of the Kiwanis club. I planned to challenge him at our next meeting. But something happened before I had my opportunity. I was informed that the manager, after closing the hotel for the evening, went out to his favorite roadside house, an extension of Third Street. When he entered the door, his special woman, a Negro, called him out publicly, and lit into him for his new policy of denying Negro customers' service. It appears she especially spoke on my behalf. I did not know the woman and vice versa. But she knew about me and my status in the community. There was my soul sister speaking up for me and other Black brothers and sisters showing our "soulfulness" that connected us. Retrospectively, as we would say today in a sermon, from an unexpected pulpit came the truth that Black Lives Do Matter.

The final story, under the topic that race matters and how I witnessed it, was brought home to me by young White students who showed how racial prejudice and discrimination touched their lives.

When the Minot High School basketball team advanced to the state tournament in Grand Forks, a handful of my Y teens encouraged me to drive them there for this extraordinary event. Many Y students and adults were among those cheering on their home team. The deal was that I would reserve a hotel room for the four or five traveling with me. They were willing to give me one bed and the others flipped for the other bed. The rest would sleep on the floor. The following morning, we went down the street to a dingy small café for breakfast. The one person there, the owner or manager, walked around the counter and took everyone's order except mine. Finally, two of my guys, the scrappy ones who became leaders, Blore and Leigh, caught on and asked what was up and why had I been refused service. He said he didn't serve Negroes. My guys went into action and told him that if he did not serve me, they would tear the place apart so much so, he wouldn't recognize it. He served me.

Teachable moments can occur in such encounters. And the teens did not pursue it on the trip back to Minot. The issue was never mentioned, but there were lots of quiet moments on our return trip. I do cherish that moment, even without knowing what my guys were thinking...

My service at the Minot YMCA was a two-way learning experience. Our overall staff consisted of the Executive Secretary, Everett Miller, Physical Education and swimming instructor, Don Anderson, business manager, Armand Lynner, Mrs. Marcell Sharkey, office manager and wife to Rev. Pops Sharkey, plus housekeeping staff for our dorms and maintenance manager and keeper of the locker rooms and pool, Bill Grunberg, often known by me as grumpy Grunberg, but a great team player! Several students from Minot State Teacher's College often found part time work on the Y staff as well as being advisors to some of our teen clubs.

I could not have been more fortunate in being offered this position. It, again, complemented those primary aspects of my ministry, pastoring, and social concerns. Since I primarily had always enjoyed working with teenagers, I saw a path in which all the above could be easily incorporated.

My predecessor left behind a solid program for our teens, for which I was grateful. It was my joy to understand the philosophy, all that was taking place and search out the best by consulting with the advisors as well as the youth themselves.

During this process of learning my way around both the Y and the community, in somewhat of a muted manner the scourge of race began to crop up.

It turned up unexpectedly through my friendship with Mr. and Mrs. Joel Davy. Joel was principal of the Minot High School and well respected in the community. Before my time in town, the nationally renowned Black news columnist and writer, Carl Rowan, delivered a lecture in Minot. And as luck would have it, he had to stay over before moving on to his next engagement. The Davys hosted a reception in their home for several educators and leaders in the community. That event would come up, time and again, in such a way that it afforded individuals and small groups opportunities to speak about the great speech Mr. Rowan delivered. And parallel to that, it gave them the opportunity to talk about race in my presence, eliciting my responses. They were muted, but direct, as I realized most dialogue was not hostile. It was simply seeking guidance and understanding as race loomed front and center throughout the nation.

The second scourge of race, far more damaging and unexpected, was when a handful of students, individually, would come to my office, close the door, and share their burden. It boiled down to the fact that their parents demanded they, the student, withdraw his/her membership from the Y due to my presence as Youth Program Secretary having sway over their children.

These individual moments were quite emotional. Without a break in their story, with heads bowed and red/flushed faces, the most onerous statement that followed was, "My father spends most of his free time down on Third Street with Negro prostitutes." Building around these statements of confession, I could only allow the student to work out this issue for himself/herself and make a paramount decision which affected their lives in more ways than race.

I am proud to say the students who came to grips with this issue began to work things out and defied the parental mandate. They remained a member of the Y and continued with their peers, whom I doubt ever knew about this personal dilemma/crisis.

I am sure this troublesome crisis concerning my race and my presence affected even more of the students, but it never reached me directly.

My overview of this and the work on race that I did prior to coming to the Y with other White young people and adults, was that teens were far more liberal, accepting, and open to multiculturalism on their own, provided they had not been tainted by parents or other adults in their lives. And in my Minot Y situation, I could simply say these young people felt once again that they had taken the high ground when it came to racial understanding and acceptance of me. They rejected or ignored their parental objections. Perhaps a John Lewis idea of "good trouble" outshined their parents in this issue.

And so it went. These were the two trigger points that followed me and my work. Everett Miller probably took the brunt of more jokes, jabs, and direct dissatisfaction concerning my appointment, since he was the face of the Y. As you can see or imagine, this was a "big deal" in 1957 in a somewhat isolated small city, out on the Prairie closer to the Canadian border than other parts of the state. It was a place where seeing a Negro was either on the movie screen or TV. There was simply little frame of reference for civil rights and all that was transpiring in the "Lower 48" about the lynching, marching, non-violent demonstrations, and more to come.

There were Hi-Y, Tri-Hi-Y clubs for the four years in high school and Junior Hi-Y programs for Junior High School boys, together numbering between twelve and fifteen. There was a Senior High-Y Counsel composed of a delegate from each club. They gave oversight to all the clubs, especially when engaged in all club events and decision making, setting policy guidelines, and earning money for special projects. Each club had an adult or college student advisor. A couple of clubs had a team of advisors. They were committed to the study of social projects, service to the community, religious aspects, and social events of their own, like dances or parties; and each club could have a one overnight lockdown in the building, with activities, food and fun. At times some clubs might have seemed like sororities and fraternities, but we kept an eye on that to make sure that was not the culture and that all students were welcomed and admitted.

Building upon the strengths left by my predecessor, I also began sharing some of my programmatic ideas. Of course, there were both successful events and ideas as well as failures.

When speaking with former staff, advisors, and youth, we often laugh, realizing that what we managed to pull off back in the 1950's certainly would not fly these days. Y youth membership consisted of those who came solely for the physical fitness center, like swimming, gym, basketball, working out and more. And there were those who took in some of the above, but also wanted to be a part of the enriched club programs. And, of course, there were the tough guys, wearing their black leather jackets, who were often the disturbers and social event crashers. My job was to get to know them all, as much as possible, keep an open-door policy in my office and work at recruiting for the Hi-Y enrichment programs at the same time.

Two of my Hi-Y club leaders and stand- out students at the Y during my tenure were Bill Blore and Ken Leigh. They would tell you at the drop of a hat that, if I had any success in running the Y's youth program, it was definitely because of them! Here is how they became a vital part of my Y work.

In my early days, a couple of Ev Miller's Y's Mens Club spoke to Miller about these two high school students who lived in their neighborhood. It was reported that they were "scrapers" and always ready to duke it out. The spokesman said what great guys they were, and he only wished they would put some of that fighting energy into one of the Y programs. Ev challenged me to get to know these guys and to see what it would portend. They were most often on the outer fringe of our activities looking in, perhaps to start a brawl.

I had the good fortune of reaching out to these two students, marginally involved, who had a reputation as scrappers, as I mentioned. But they had real leadership qualities. They often eyed me with cynicism, doubt and a "prove it to me" attitude.

I got a fix on them. They eyed me and vice versa. Since Ev Miller and I always kept an open-door policy in our offices, one day they ventured into the office, introduced themselves and wanted to know more about me and my plans for the Y's youth programs, because they had ideas they felt had been overlooked and that they had not been taken seriously. I considered their thinking about becoming more closely involved.

From that point forward, we managed to chat, either in the Y-Grill or in my office and they enjoyed both the attention and the fact that I listened attentively enough to take some of their aspirational goals seriously. Before long, their Hi-Y club reflected many of their ideas and ideals they shared with me. To cut to the chase, they ultimately found themselves inside of the circle in accepting leadership roles and pushing some of their agenda. Ev and the person who passed along the story were both pleased and felt that was what the Y was all about.

Blore and Leigh became my star or best leaders. They continued sharing ideas they felt had not been investigated, never missed dropping in my office or inviting me to the Grill for coffee, a coke or dialogue. In essence, they became my eyes and ears for much of the Y's programs – they had my back. And there were times, believe me, when I was more than grateful. They knew how to duke it out with obstreperous, rowdy characters and could take on any. Strangely enough, that was not my image of them.

As our relationships bonded, they, and some of their close friends, felt both protective of me and desirous to get to know me better. So much so that they invited themselves to take a trip with me to Chicago for an emergency I had to deal with. They shared driving and were excited about seeing a real big city.

They were natural leaders (with a bit) of guidance and enjoyed that role. Blore became the interim Y youth director upon my departure and did an outstanding job. Following college, he had a fine tenure, over thirty years as director of Court Services, N.W. District of N.D., focusing on juvenile services.

I had the honor of officiating at Ken Leigh's marriage to the love of his life and loaned them my car for their honeymoon. However, they had only driven twenty + miles before a blizzard came up, so they hunkered down at the nearest motel and returned the next day or so to Minot. Ken also distinguished himself in becoming the executive officer for several Chambers of Commerce in and around North Dakota and beyond. We have never been out of touch, sixty years later.

To make it short, they became involved and ultimately were two of my best student leaders. They always had my back and participated on a deeper level than most. Ev Miller, who had pointed them out, was taken aback and said I needed an A+ for engendering that type of leadership.

Here are some **Program Highlights** from my tenure that point out just how committed and involved these youngsters were on all levels.

INTERNATIONAL YMCA YOUTH GATHERING in Amsterdam. Upon receiving the invitation to send two delegates, the Hi-Y Council decided to accept the invitation, develop a selection process, and raise the money to send two of our finest and best to that international gathering. Each club committed itself to help in fund raising. My great all-club fund raiser idea was to have a Bar-B-Q at the local park and cash in on the funds. We did all the right things, had expert help from the Y's Men's Club with a couple of great chefs who helped prepare, cook and distribute the great food. It worked out well, but didn't catch on throughout the community. I spent the next week selling marinated spareribs, chunks of beef, uncooked hamburger meat and more. The students were in school and therefore could not help me take on that task. A bust! My one candid and most insightful advisor, Vivian Maragos, warned me from the beginning that she had doubts about the success of such an event. She was right.

Funds were raised, the students went to Amsterdam and returned with an outstanding report, as I recall.

BOYS CHOIR – Ev Miller had organized a Barbershop Quartet that performed in various places in the city. At one point, he suggested I organize a Boys' Choir, the likes of which he had seen and heard in YMCA's in the Twin Cities. In our monthly newsletter, I placed a blurb concerning this event where boys between nine and twelve could sign up at the Y. Not thinking this would go anywhere, or was just wishful thinking on my part, I was overwhelmed to see the list at the front desk fill up with about twenty kids.

I reached out to one of my former Berthold church pianists, Verna De-Bilt, now a student at Minot State Teacher's College. For a small fee, she became my accompanist for the Minot Y Boys Choir. They were energetic and had a penchant for music. But it was hard to keep their attention. With my big voice, and color, I suppose, they toed the line and we had fun in learning new songs and even performing for the Y's Annual Meeting and a few other places.

The **BIG KAHUNA** came when some of the boy's mothers caught the ad in the Minot Daily News that the Vienna Boys' Choir was coming to town for a performance. The mothers ganged up on me in my office and insisted we provide hospitality for a potluck supper with our choir boys and they could all get to know each other. Of course, the Vienna boys spoke little English, but that didn't matter. The mothers also insisted that our choir sing a number for them at the dinner and they, in turn would honor us with one of their renditions. All of this was passed by the Vienna director and manager. They were delighted! I was somewhat hesitant and anxious, given this internationally acclaimed choir, whereas we sang camp and folk songs.

The mothers were right. It was a grand evening until each choir serenaded the other. We did our thing, but the Vienna sound had that angelic quality of professionalism that, once you heard it, the sound lingered, and you felt you had died and gone to heaven. Several of us attended their concert at the Minot Auditorium the following evening. It was a great experience for my group and their mothers and families.

Too often, with joy comes sadness. Two of the choir members were brothers, less than a year apart, perhaps twins, I can't recall. On Labor Day, before school started, they were riding on one bike when another Y high school senior was in his basement cleaning his gun, preparing it for hunting season. Out of his basement window, he focused his aim on the garage handle across the street, pulled the trigger at the same instant that the brothers were riding by. The gun was loaded, no one knows why, and one of the brothers was killed instantly.

This became a teachable moment for our choir members and the wider community. Of course, the Y Boys' Choir sang for the service. This was one of the most difficult periods in their lives, as well as in mine.

THE YOUTH COMMITTEE - Ev and I concluded at one of our staff meetings, how important it would be to have a committee of about fifteen adults; parents, educators and other lay people to serve as a sounding board for our teen programs and projects. All well and good, thought I.

One of the most critical issues I faced, along with my adult club advisors, was that so many of our teens were "going steady." From my observation and counseling, I placed before the committee the need for a responsible sex education program, including perhaps a doctor, psychologist, member of the clergy and so forth. For all the good ideas and suggestions the Youth Committee was known for, they voted solidly "No" on sex education. I lost this one!

INTERNATIONAL HI-Y & TRI-Y EXCHANGE WEEKENDS - I believe this was in place under my predecessor. The closest Y to Minot was the YMCA of Regina, Saskatchewan, Canada. My ol' stomping grounds, in my 1940's hitchhiking days, of all places. They extended an invitation for our senior Hi-Y club members for an international exchange visit. We would go to Regina one weekend and later they would come and visit us for a weekend. This was another great idea for teachable opportunities in international relations. I, along with two advisors, chaperoned a bus load of students to Regina and later that year, they sent their teens to Minot.

Managing international protocol with our teens was a joy and helpful in ways they never expected, such as learning their national anthem, plus "God save the Queen," a bit of Canadian history and the issues pertinent to Saskatchewan, a province not too unlike North Dakota, just above us. They leaned towards a more formal lifestyle unlike North Dakota in many ways. Great teachable opportunities.

ALL HI-Y, TRI-HI-Y AND JR. HI-Y CLUB SUNDAY GATHERINGS. I am not sure how this came into play, but suspect it was one of Ev Miller's ideas he had experienced in Minneapolis. The concept was that all clubs would come together for a student-planned Sunday afternoon, Vesper-like time in a local church, to showcase their programs, club by club, song fest, and end with a message from the host pastor. It was putting the "C" back in the YMCA. We even sang hymns and read scripture. This was quite successful and well attended. In my opinion, few churches had traditional youth programs, but the YMCA filled that need for many church-going teens. Of course, they had confirmation classes and other ways of dealing with the young people in their congregations. Our Y programs were somewhat like a church youth group. Many mainline clergy were active members of the Y along with their families.

The workload was heavy. As the students continued to show confidence in me and my leadership, I was often swamped as many came to my office after school and before club meetings in the evenings. There were meetings with club advisors and keeping tabs on their work and progress. There was genuine mutual respect in planning, discussing events at school, personal counseling, family affairs and more. With all of this, I managed some free time and opportunities to get involved in the other aspect of my assignment, namely, meeting with groups and organizations outside of the Y and, where opportunities presented themselves to take on speaking assignments. With all of the time and effort I poured into this job, it was an asset to be single.

My social life was fine, all things considered. I usually hung out with folk who invited me to meals at their homes, teachers and parents of Y students and an assortment of others. At one point two Black couples were assigned to the US Radar station south of town. I got to know them, and we often partied together and enjoyed having joyful "soulful" gatherings where we could let our hair down, be ourselves and compare experiences, especially related to race in or around Minot.

One of my good friends from my home church in Chicago, Al Sampson, Negro, and graduate of Grinnell College, was looking for work in his field of journalism and English. I managed to get him a job as a proofreader (I think that was his title) at the Minot Daily News. It worked well, except his skin was so light, he blended in with the rest of the staff. And some wondered where the Negro was that Polk encouraged us to hire! Al remained only a few months before receiving a scholarship for graduate school at the University of Chicago.

The clergy association extended me a wonderful invitation to be guest preacher on World Communion Sunday, the first Sunday in October, at an ecumenical service. It was here that I was expected to do my thing and speak to issues of brotherhood, race relations, and social justice or along that line.

Three days prior to this long-expected event, a Lt. Roland Davis had been assigned to the Minot Air Base. He checked in at the Y and I made it my business to greet him and try to get to know him. That's what I did with other Negro airmen who came to the base and lived in our Y dormitories until housing was made available at the air base.

On Lt. Davis' second night in Minot, we shared dinner out and got to know each other. At that time, I was living in a basement apartment of the Episcopal parsonage. The rector and his family were fine landlords, and we were friends.

Lt. Davis made an unusual request that evening. He asked if he could room with me and sleep on the couch in my living room until the Bachelor Quarters for officers at the base were available. I agreed that it was not a problem whatsoever. Many others had shared that living room couch in days past.

Davis had one of the most beautiful and unusual cars Minot folks had seen, a teal blue convertible MG. The kids at the Y were enamored. North Dakotans would never have a convertible, for weather purposes. Davis had driven it from his base in Texas.

I spent most of my time Sunday preparing for my World Communion Sermon on the second floor of the Y where our club rooms were so I would not be disturbed. When I arrived home late in the afternoon to shower, shave and dress for the church service, Davis was not there. One of my Y students called to chat and expressed his sadness about my roommate. When I expressed my unawareness of his statement, he said he hated to be the first to tell me that Lt. Davis was killed driving his car on a road near the Radar Station south of town. He hit gravel and turned over three times. There was a neighbor junior high school student with him who was not killed but hospitalized.

This shook me to the very core of my existence, especially since I was about to preach. The radio station carried the news, and it was all over town. I attended the service as if a zombie, expressions of condolences were offered by the clergy. I went on but have no idea what I preached or how it went. I simply wanted to get home, collect my thoughts as I attempted to learn the entire story. Good friend, David Waldron, called and offered to come over and spend the night with me and see me through the next day when the Air Force officers came for Davis' belongings and a statement. My landlord/clergyman upstairs and family were also helpful through the next few days. The kid with Davis was a next-door neighbor and remained in the hospital a few days, I guess. Everything from there on was a blur.

The Minot Daily News account was okay, as I recall. However, years later in writing the paper for a copy of that accident, it was noticeable that they left out that Davis had a passenger and referred to it as a single car accident and only the driver, no passenger, as I recall.

Lt. Davis was from Bristol, PA. I wrote a letter of condolence to the family, Later I visited them. And his mother sent me a marvelous letter informing me how the family was doing and a copy of Roland's memorial service. I have managed to keep in touch with the family over the years. There is only one sister living in Bristol and we communicate periodically.

Being race sensitive as I am, I attributed the article and report to the tenor and tone which began in Minot as Air Base staff came in large numbers and I witnessed the anti-Negro attitude building around town as some of the Negro airmen who came through the Y expressed to me.

I even had my first taste of Minot's bigotry towards Negro airmen in particular. At issue for me was how to call it out? A few I had gotten to know upon their arrival would stop in my office and share their pain. Others would talk to Mrs. Sharkey when paying their dorm room rent at the YMCA.

Early on in my work at the Minot Y, Ev Miller called me into his office. He had authorized Armend Lynner, our business manager, to send a check to the Minot Kiwanis Club for me to become a member. I knew little about those luncheon clubs but I was aware that Ev was a member of the Rotary Club.

The deal was that the board of trustees of the Y felt it was important for the executive director of the Y to become a Rotarian and the Youth Sec-retary to be a Kiwanian.

All was well with that decision and the president of the Kiwanis Club called to welcome me with open arms. He expected me to attend the next meeting where I would, along with several others, be inducted as new members.

I attended the meeting, was introduced, and then hosted by several older members, making sure I felt welcomed at their weekly luncheon club. Many of the men I already knew from their membership and activity in the YMCA. Once I caught on, I made friends with a cadre of guys with whom I sat at their table for lunch at most meetings. I learned about the club, its national and international involvement in social and philanthropic work, as well as their important endeavors in Minot.

The club's philosophy/rules were that you are never to miss a meeting, regardless of where you are, unless it was an emergency. All club members seemed to adhere to that concept. Whenever traveling, they would locate a Kiwanis Club nearby and attend that meeting. In that way they would receive credit at their home club. I wish that churches could be so didactic and precise about membership and attendance!

I was to be back home in Chicago on my vacation, visiting my parents and siblings. Knowing nothing about a Kiwanis Club there, I agreed with my local president that I would visit the brand-new headquarters of Kiwanis in Chicago. That would satisfy my not missing a club meeting and I could report back about my visit to the new headquarters.

I diligently did all that was required. I entered the national offices and was warmly met by the surprised receptionist. When I presented my Kiwanis credentials, she notified the person in charge – perhaps the president or some high official. He welcomed me and took me on a tour of the building. It was a pleasant experience and then I headed back to the South Side of Chicago to be with my family and friends.

When I returned to Minot, I had an urgent call from our Minot Kiwanis club leader. He could not wait to stop in and visit with me to inform me of the many calls and letters they had from the Kiwanis national office, following my visit. At issue was that the national office had been flooded with requests from local clubs about accepting Negro members: what was the policy and how should they proceed? There apparently was no national policy and each club had to make its own decision. Therefore, they wondered, what process was used in Minot to accept me as a member.

My club executives fired back and said there was no process and explained they followed the policy of the YMCA of a commitment to diversity, equity, inclusion and engagement. All of which leads me to say that there I was again, building bridges. I believe that, perhaps, I became the first Negro Kiwanian in the country. There was no big deal accepting me in the Minot club, as they understood it. White Kiwanis members in Minot seemed quite welcoming. Perhaps I was that fly in the buttermilk again.

Once I left Minot, I no longer maintained my Kiwanis Club membership.

That attitude was so different in my early life. In looking back to childhood and the predominantly Black community in which I was reared, White men always had a dubious and nefarious pres-ence. A few were legitimately married to Negro women. Some were bill and insurance collectors, and so forth, whom we were told "made whoopee" with our Negro women, single or married. And some were fly-by-nights who preyed upon Negro girls and women. Mind you, Black men in those days had little or no power or status to stand up to them. It didn't take long to recognize sandy-headed children running around the neigh-borhood from some of these White characters. Unfortunately, my socio-logical background is not significant enough to provide more in-depth information about this situation. We need only to look to some of our Founding Fathers, like Thomas Jefferson, for the real historic take on such actions.

On a lighter note, a first-generation Norwegian farmer, with a son in the Saturday Y swimming program, took a shine to me as he dropped into my office for chats while his boy was learning to swim. On a couple of oc-casions, he invited me to a stag Norwegian smorgasbord gathering – fea-turing great food and drink—prepared by the women, of course. It was an all-afternoon affair. He loved introducing me to his friends as the Black Norwegian. I enjoyed the food and the fellowship!

One dish they especially wanted my reaction to was Rocky Mountain Oysters—exquisitely prepared sheep or bull testicles. This was their big surprise. They were immediately wondering what I thought once they iden-tified the dish. What I didn't tell them in return was that, in my Black community, we ate chitterlings (the bowel lining of the pig). So there!

Returning to the Y youth programs, there were two exceptional events that might have been key to my administration and programing.

Our youth memberships were high and club groups were full. There was no place for large teen gatherings for sox hops, dances or simply places to gather, considering the numbers. This was a matter to be considered. In one of our weekly staff conferences, Ev had come up with a plan. He took me down to the unfinished basement under the Y and said that perhaps we can find a way to make use of this ample, unused space and turn it into a multipurpose room for our teenagers. It looked doable and good to me, and he took the idea to his board of directors, who gave approval and,

I think, offered to put financial resources behind their approval, once we developed a budget and a plan.

I took the idea before the Hi-Y and Tri-Hi-Y Council and there was candid interest in this. They were concerned, however, about how this space could be a place for them, off the beaten path, with no windows and so forth. I think we sketched out a plan and the reality set in. It was given the green light by the council and put forth into all the clubs. The clubs would help raise money for the project, which was in their self-interest.

It became a cause celebre and, before long, several groups were in support of the project by offering funds, in-kind service, professional service and offers of volunteer labor. The Y's Men's Club pitched in with some of their contracting and members who were contractors. The labor union hall was next-door to the Y and they offered help with plumbing, electrical installations, wall paneling, stucco ceilings and more. The well-loved and popular shop teacher, along with several of his students, offered to build the control center/operation at the front door. And it all came into fruition. Dating back to WWII, for lack of a better name, it was simply called The Y Canteen. It was highly successful and greatly appreciated!

The second project was one of those iconic events, one would never venture to try in this century, with twenty-two Junior High boys from Minot.

One day, before the end of the lunch hour, per usual the Y was full of kids in the Y-Grill or playing ping pong or just lounging about. My office door was open and in popped Joey Jacobson, a Junior High student. Junior High kids never sit down. They usually plop down. This was Joey's posture when he started asking me questions. He had observed that both Ev Miller and I had Sloane House YMCA calendars on our walls and wondered what it was and where was it located. I told him it was like a mega YMCA Hotel in New York City. He next asked me, "Bob, do you think our club could ever go to New York City?" I was taken aback, but didn't miss a beat and said, "Yes, why not." He said, "I'll tell our club at its next meeting." And he left the office the same way he came in.

A day or two later, following Joey's Junior Hi-Y Club meeting, I guess he told the club what I had said. His club advisor, a Junior High School teacher (Robert Jadg), came to my office infuriated and scolded me for putting such ideas into the club, knowing full-well that it was not possible.

I hit back and told him I thought it was doable and invited him to come to my place for dinner the next night with a bottle of wine and we could discuss the possibility. He did and the trip was on!

I made the case by pointing out one or two of the many fund raiser pamphlets the Y receives monthly. The one that looked the best was a box of thin mints. A box would cost thirty-three cents. Club members could sell the boxes for one dollar. Each boy could get fifty cents per box, thirty-three cents to the company and seventeen cents for Y advisors. Furthermore, we could make this not only a fun holiday trip, but a profound learning experience for each student. The teacher liked that.

To cut to the chase, he divided his twenty-two students into study groups about the trip of how we would get there, costs, housing at the Sloane House Y, places to see and things to do. Each club member would sell as many boxes of mints as necessary to make the trip, and, in some cases, subsidized by several joyous but cautious parents – whom I had to convince.

It was a go! The Minot Daily News gave us a lead story with a photo of several boys sitting on a mountain of thin mint boxes. Many of the kids were innate hustlers and sold boxes in excess of the amount needed. That went to their personal slush fund for entertainment and more. There was even enough money for me to hire a high school student to accompany us and be the go-between and another two eyes and ears for the boys.

These teachable moments and study clusters all worked perfectly well, beginning with the Station Master of the CB&Q RR about the train route, costs, days, and times as well as places and pleasures in the Big Apple such as a Yankee game with the home-boy Roger Maris, a North Dakotan, whom we tried to contact for a ball signing, but to no avail. Also on the docket of possibilities was a trip to the U.N. and a visit to the Statue of Liberty. One team contacted a Minot student, Phil Costain, a West Point Military Academy cadet to see if he could host us. He graciously agreed, and we spent half a day visiting the academy, with Phil Costain as our guide.

We spent one Sunday in New York City and I made the executive decision to attend Riverside Church, which I had never seen but heard about and read about during my seminary career. This was the iconic historic "Baptist" cathedral-like church in Manhattan, built by John D. Rockefeller, Jr. I knew our ND boys had never seen a cathedral, so we went to worship there.

We always traveled in lines of twos. The advisor was at the head of the line, the high school student in the middle, and I brought up the rear. When we reached the doors of this massive building, the likes of which none had ever seen in North Dakota or elsewhere, the word got back to me, "Bob what kind of church is this, the ushers asked if we had reservations? The answer was no. So, they sent us up to the second balcony, via elevator. And, even there, we could not all sit together due to the vast numbers of worshippers. The nave of the church could seat about three thousand people.

It was the first Sunday in June 1960, and a communion Sunday. They served communion in individual silver-like chalices. And there were racks in the pew in front of you to place the cups there at the end of the service. Some of my guys had purchased binoculars and looked down on the service from their seats.

I gave each of my two counselors a day off during our excursion. My day off would be Monday, following the Sunday at Riverside and the visit to the Statue of Liberty.

All went well to this point. We did all the things tourists do when visiting the Statue of Liberty, like going up into the crown, or simply walking the many stairs. We had return tickets on the ferry at a specific time. When it was time to board the ferry, one boy was missing. No one seemed to know where Peterson was, even after a short search. We had to take that ferry, and we did. For the first time, the group felt a sense of being united and looking out for each other. They were worried about Peterson and angry with me for going forward without him.

We reached Sloan House Y in time for our five o'clock dinner, for which we had paid. They had set us up in a small dining room. All the guys were paying attention, still worried about what had happened to their lost buddy.

Half-way through the meal, who should come storming through the double doors to the dining room but Peterson, face all red and crying his heart out (great applause from the group)! A united sigh of relief went throughout the dining room. From that point forward, no one, and I mean no one, missed a gathering or broke rank! It was good youth or group work technique, making one example when the group gets a bit careless. It worked.

My day off on Monday was spent having lunch with my seminary classmate, Andrew Young, his wife Jean and two daughters. Andy was working
for the National Council of Churches doing church youth ministry (UCYM)
on the East Coast. At one point in our reunion and luncheon, he asked
when I was going to leave North Dakota and return to civilization. It was
somewhat of a throwaway line, and I said, "As soon as an opportunity in a
church presents itself."

On our return trip to Minot, in the wee hours of the morning, one student awakened me and told me he needed to talk and that what he had to
say, I must promise not to tell anyone in the group. I asked if it could not
wait until we reached Minot? He said no and commenced telling me that
four of the guys in our group had stolen communion cups from Riverside
Church.

I sat up immediately and was wide awake! I promised at that point I
would not say anything. I was aghast! What a burden and how could I
wrap my mind around such a story without calling attention to the theft
and the implications for my young Y boys?

We arrived in Minot on time. Parents, siblings, the mayor, the station
master, and Ev Miller and a few others were there to meet and greet their
wonderful kids. That is not what I would have called them, given the information regarding the communion cup episode.

Of course, the mothers wanted to plan a potluck gathering for the boys
to talk about their experience. In a few days, the plans were set. But my
mind was still on the communion cups and how I should handle the situation. This required more than a teachable moment. I don't believe I even
told the club advisor or the high school student. In hindsight, I thought,
what if they had been Black kids? Would the church ushers in their fancy
cut-a ways, stripped trousers, carnations, and white gloves have noticed
the missing cups and stopped us before we exited the building? How do I
make this a teachable moment, especially when I do not know who the
boys were and promised not to tell? I allowed for this to marinate a few
days, while I planned to take another Y younger group up to a YMCA camp
for a canoe trip in that pristine wilderness country near Ely, MN. It was
too beautiful to miss, and we were invited to join a group of Minneapolis
YMCA boys whose camp it was. I looked forward to this contrast from NYC

and had set my mind on the trip.

The day before my long-awaited canoe trip, I received a letter from The Riverside Church. My heart skipped a beat or two and, if I could have turned red, all the signs would have been there. I was deeply embarrassed and, without opening it, knew what it was about. I decided to place the letter, unopened, at the back of my desk, deliver my troop of kids for their first canoe trip, and open the letter from Riverside upon my return.

Back at the office, that Riverside Church letter, though at the back of the desk, seemed to be staring directly at me, demanding it be opened, even though I knew the news was awful – all about communion cups my little monsters had taken.

To the contrary, the letter had nothing to do with the communion cups, but was an inquiry asking if I would be interested in a job as Minister to Youth at the church? I was relieved, overwhelmed, and quietly wept following the second reading. Feeling I probably would not be their finalist, I still had great joy just in the prospect of Riverside looking at me for the job.

Following my instincts, and not wanting to divulge this information to Ev Miller or other staff members, I hightailed it up to Joel and Helen Davys' to discuss the opportunities, of finding me and placing me among one who was engaged in creative youth work.

Joel Davy was not home, so Helen and I waded through the pros and cons and what it might mean for me, should I be their choice. But what about the communion cups, I asked? Deal with that later, said Helen. We drafted a response to their letter and within days, the Youth Committee of the church made contact and invited me to come to the church for an in-person interview. And I finally shared the proposal with Ev Miller and others.

To explain this more clearly, I went via Chicago to share the news with my parents and siblings before heading up to New York City. I was only to be there overnight, meet with the search committee and return to Chicago and back to Minot.

The church's Youth Committee had devised a unique interviewing plan for the job. They had five candidates and divided the committee up into five small groups. Each group met a candidate somewhere in the church or in the homes of committee members. At the end of the process, they all gath-

ered for dinner at the church to share their findings. Each group made its
report and evaluation. Apparently, I came out on top. I was asked by the chair,
a deacon and professor of Law at Columbia University, to remain over one
more day to meet the ministerial staff for their chance to meet me and, hopefully, give their approval, along with one final meeting with the chair to clinch
the deal. This indicated that the position was mine if I agreed.

All of this worked so fast, my head was swimming. I had not even prepared for a second night and day in New York but kept my room at the
New Yorker Hotel and headed back to Minot with the GOOD NEWS!

And, by the way, no member of the committee or clergy ever made mention of the communion cups. I felt relieved.

It was mid-August! The church wanted me there ASAP, but I had to
clean up my work at the Y. Although my resignation did not meet the re-
quirement of a thirty-day warning, I managed to work everything out with
the grace of Ev Miller, my Youth Committee and others in light of this great
venture I was to undertake. From right out of the Minot YMCA, Polk would
be the first Negro to serve on the ministerial staff of the church John D.
Rockefeller, Jr. built. This, in a current phrase, was a "Big Deal," not only
for Minot folk, my family, home church and for many others across the
inter-church spectrum and especially Black persons. Another fly in a larger
bottle of buttermilk!

This appointment did not just happen out of the ether. Let's take a step
back for context. My day off in NYC, when my Junior Hi-Y guys went out
to see the Yankees play ball, I spent lunch and the afternoon with my fellow
seminary classmate, Andrew Young and his wife and family. Andy had been
working for the National Council of Churches in their youth division,
pumping up local and regional church youth programs in the northeast.
Riverside members, who knew of his gifts and the fine work he was doing,
asked if he would be interested in the Youth Ministry job which had recently become vacant. Andy indicated he and his wife, Jean, had already
committed themselves to go to South and work for Dr. Martin Luther King,
Jr. and S.C.L.C. Those who approached Andy had asked him for names of
youth leaders he observed doing great work with teenagers and whose
names he could pass along to the search committee. He provided them
with six or seven names and mine was one of the names on his list. The

rest is history. And, by the way, this is the same Andrew Young appointed by President Jimmy Carter to become the U.S. Delegate to the United Nations, a former Congressman and former Mayor of Atlanta, GA. We have remained friends and in touch over the years.

Earlier in this memoir, I mentioned another, unexpected, return to North Portal, North Dakota. Here's what happened. During my last year at the Y, as is true to this day, I don't spend much time-sharing stories, or talking about myself. So, one day my boss, Ev Miller, came to my office telling me of an invitation to the dedication of the new YMCA in Regina, Saskatchewan, Canada. Ev said this was the closest Y to us and we should make the trip. All of which I had known when our seniors had that exchange weekend together. I was only too glad to agree. Along the way, as we were getting close to Portal, ND. I started telling Ev of my experience hitchhiking to Canada with a Chicago buddy and how we crossed over through this very border station back in 1947.

I went on to embellish that story by telling how we met the Premier of Saskatchewan, became friends, and rode with him to the CCF convention in Saskatoon and more. Ev seemed so interested that I topped it off by saying I would not be surprised if Premier T.C. Douglas would be the keynote speaker for this event. I noted what it would mean to me to revisit my former stomping grounds with its new building. By this time, Ev gave me a ho-hum glance.

We arrived at the new Y, checked in and had time for a snack before the main event. When we were handed the program, I scanned it and learned that the dedicatory address would be delivered by none other than Premier T.C. Douglas. Ev nudged me and winked and smiled, likely rethinking my story and how much it resonated with him.

At the end of the event, I took Ev to join the long line wishing to speak to Mr. Douglas. When we reached Mr. Douglas, I introduced myself with a brief recall of our meeting in 1947. He said, "Oh yes, I remember you. And how is your friend?" He was speaking of Doug Kelley.

I introduced him to Ev, told him of my work in Minot and the YMCA, and a bit more. Ev was deeply impressed. And that was the key story, when we returned to Minot, about meeting the Premier, whom Bob had known in another life.

The Riverside Church

From Minot To Manhattan!

SOME MIGHT ASK WHAT my major regret about might be leaving so abruptly. Yes, my departure from Minot was before school reopened in September. I was unable to meet with my Junior High group that I helped chaperone to New York City. I felt the need for a debriefing with that group. But that wasn't possible. If I could go back and do two things about that group, I would do two things. First, I would affirm the totality of the experience with them about how finely they comported themselves and all worked together so well. Secondly, I would have followed up with a "come to Jesus" moment of the communion cups of Riverside church and make that an important ethical conversation for all to consider now and in their future lives.

Once again, this new job at Riverside, though daunting, made use of my parallel and special gifts: a devotion to the gospel of Jesus Christ in my ministry and my passion for social justice and race relations.

The Riverside job embraced all of this and more as it began to see itself not as a silk-stocking, lily-white, wealthy captains of industry institutional church with unlimited resources to work with. It saw the need to reorder its image and priorities and provide a stronger ministry to the immediate community, namely Harlem and beyond, and attracting, especially Asian, Black, Caucasian, Hispanic young people and more to its programs. My job was to create a multi-phased program that embraced all such young people representing not only ethnic backgrounds, but social, economic, and academic aspects as well. This was an arduous task!

I closed out my Minot responsibilities. There were a few, on the spot, farewells, one with the Y staff and co-workers, and abundant good wishes. Having just seen Porgy and Bess on the big screen with fellow Y co-workers a few weeks earlier, before all of this took place, I felt like Porgy's on his last, great solo, going to New York to find his Bess, singing, "O Lord, I'm on my way…" And so, it was. I left Minot with good credentials and a fine record both for my work and community input.

In my form of work, when one leaves a position, there is usually little if any residual connection with those left behind, those with whom you have spent so much time and shared deeply with each other.

In leaving Minot, the rush and hurriedness of my departure in late August provided little time for deep farewells with Y staff or Y teens, still on summer vacation. When some Minot businessmen, at the end of a cruise, came to pay a brief visit and to see Riverside Church, I felt that was perhaps the last I would hear or visit anyone from my North Dakota past in perhaps months, if not years.

Not so! For the decades which followed my tenure out there, I have had a series of wonderful, sustainable contacts with Y students, leaders, and friends from that short period.

All of which has led me to believe that my time there, regardless of my race, was not an anomaly and that the relationships were genuine and impactful.

So let me highlight what I mean about ongoing relationships.

At holiday times, there were cards, notes and letters, long before emails, that warmed the cockles of my heart. Also, there were in-person visits with people some might recognize.

I have always had great love and appreciation for the people and the state because of my experiences there. That means I have remained in contact with my ND friends and have always had a high regard for what each of us gave to each other during my tenure there. And so, over these past 6 decades, I can recount several times when I felt privileged to be invited back to the state for special occasions.

I visited Berthold in 1993, when my denomination, the United Church of Christ, brought me out of retirement to work in its new initiative, Make a Difference campaign, to raise $33 million for much needed programs. I was attached to the Major Gifts part of the campaign. When it came to

Bob Polk and Edna Keiser

dividing up the country and assigning staff to various state conferences, I was the only one who had North Dakota experience and that was my assignment. I was thrilled to visit the state requesting funds for the national campaign. I traveled to Bismarck to meet with several clergy and potential lay givers. It was like a reunion gathering. All went well and that trip enabled me to see and meet old friends I had worked with in Minot.

In my first visit back to Berthold in forty years, Edna Keiser and her daughter, Kay, organized a coffee and dessert afternoon at Tumbleweed Café, one of the new cafes on Main Street. About twenty-five showed up and we responded like long lost sisters and brothers. Stories were shared and appreciation was explicit. Much had changed over the years. Edna and Kay drove me around Berthold to see all the improvements. I was amazed! My house and the church were gone. AND more importantly, there was no sign of the outhouse!

What I am stressing is that my sojourn in North Dakota was not just an anomaly. I am quite aware that it is easier for White people to accept one or a few Blacks while not necessarily changing their minds, hearts or attitudes about race or about Black people in larger numbers. On a more one-on-one basis, people may not feel anxious or threatened. On a larger context, however, can things shift?

Another visit came when the First Congregational Church of Minot celebrated its centennial. The church had been served by several pastors since I was there. The church faced some struggles with waning membership and attendance, like most mainline churches. Someone on the planning committee remembered me and made contact to see if I would be their Anniversary speaker at Sunday worship. I agreed and made all the necessary preparations.

Since we were now in the 21st century, I no longer took the CB&Q Empire Builder train from Chicago but went by air. The chair of the anniversary and his wife met me and got me registered at one of the hotels owned by the Maragos family (remember Vivian Maragos Zimmerman, superb volunteer Y leader)? I made a few calls with the hope of seeing some of the old co-workers and friends from my Y days.

The church committee did all the right things in making the town aware of the seminal event at old First Congregational through the newspaper, TV and radio. On Sunday morning, as people gathered for worship, I was amazed at the crowd that came out. Not only that, but prior to that, I had received notes and messages from friends in places where I had worked in the state, such as Garrison, the Ft. Berthold reservation and Berthold. What a gathering of friends and supporters!

I felt both humbled and privileged.

The previous night was the 100th Anniversary banquet and the organization The Red Hatters dominated. I am not sure why, but their emphasis was not on the church's anniversary.

The worship service was printed out and in proper order. The music was great, announcements and statement of purpose for this auspicious occasion. Unfortunately, the immediate former pastor could not be present at the last minute and as a result, no one was there to host, or tie the service together or even introduce me. At that point in the service when I was to preach, I simply mounted the pulpit and began to speak, congratulations the church on this momentous occasion, welcomed and greeted friends of yore, plus guest visitors. As I moved on to my text and sermon, a strange thing happened to me, I almost felt as if I could not continue the sermon. There was a chilliness and void in the words I uttered and, for better words, the sermon "tanked". I felt terribly embarrassed with so many dear ones out simply to see and hear me. I felt so embarrassed and tried not to show it. But internally, I had simply lost it and I could see registering on some of the faces I knew best. It is difficult to describe, only to point out that I have experienced this on two other occasions during my seventy years as a pastor.

None of this deterred me from having a marvelous time following the service with old friends and former teenagers. They gathered in small clusters at the hotel for coffee, spirits, and much fellowship, including Vivian Maragos Zimmerman, her husband Dudley, my former Jr. High Y advisor who took the trip to New York with his group, Bob Jadg and his wife, Ruth, and an array of others during my brief stay.

As you can tell, my time in North Dakota has resonated within me all these many years. In many ways, what I learned there has shaped my life, often in unexpected ways. And the friendships I developed remain treasures of goodness for me.

Three weeks into my Riverside tenure, I received a wire from six or eight Minot couples – shakers and movers in Minot and some trustees at the YMCA. They had been on a cruise to London and were headed back to the States. They were to arrive in NYC on a certain date and wanted to know if they could come to see me and how I was doing plus have a look at the church built by John D. Rockefeller. This was a glad surprise to have such distinguished visitors from back home.

The wives stayed behind to shop or rest, but the men hopped in two cabs and came up to Riverside on a balmy autumn afternoon as the sun was setting over the Hudson River and New Jersey. They jumped out of the cabs, keeping them waiting during their brief visit. I met them in front on Riverside Drive and took them into the church. They were simply amazed. Ushering them up to the front of the Nave, I gave them what little history I had read and picked up during my brief weeks there.

They were in awe, greeted me warmly and smiled upon leaving, as if to say, "One of our boys made it!" Indeed, I had made it, with their support and that of many others!

I have no doubt that those initial visitors had little concept of Riverside Church, its prominence and mission I was to carry out. Let me contextualize it.

It was, at that specific time, the gold standard of White, liberal, mainline (progressive) Protestant churches in America. And it was built by one of America's richest men, John D. Rockefeller Jr., who was a deeply devoted Christian and member of the Baptist denomination all his life. He even taught a men's Bible study group/class up until the end of his life. He was a great philanthropist and left an enduring legacy. Mr. Rockefeller teamed up with one of America's great preachers and progressive thinkers, Harry Emerson Fosdick. They both wanted to build a church that was interdenominational, international, and interracial to reach great numbers of God's people in New York City, thus Riverside Church. The site selected to reach a broad variety of people was Morningside Heights, often referred to as the Acropolis of America. The institutions of higher learning in that complex were: Columbia University, Teachers College, Juilliard School of Music, International House, Jewish Theological Seminary and Union Theological Seminary.

I was the church's first Black pastor and staff member out of seventy-five in 1960. Both the New York Times and the New York Harold Tribune carried the story. This was a big deal

As an aside, one of my dear fellow seminary classmates had earlier warned me not to stay in North Dakota too long or I would be dubbed as a rural pastor and never find a charge in a major city. So much for that!

Being selected from my small and failed first parish (by urban standards), and my stint at the Minot Y, it felt like going from a one-room schoolhouse to the Ivy League.

When the Minot wisemen/guests left, I mounted the steps back into the church and sat in a pew and exhaled. I needed quiet time to reflect. Everything around me seemed to be shut out — all the beauty of the vast church, its stained-glass windows, impressive altar, cross and more just disappeared. My inner reflection was about my worthiness. Was I capable of pulling off such a task assigned to me in this extraordinary cathedral-like church with all its wealth, Whiteness, captains of industry as members and leaders of the congregation? Those were the new searing issues I had to face and prove my ability, along with being, yet again, another Fly– an African American.

I, no doubt, dozed off. And the next thing I recalled was hearing the massive, largest bell of the carillon struck five. It was time for me to return to my office and continue studying the church, its founding, architecture, liberal theology and commitment to social justice and racial inclusion.

Finding my way back to my office was like going through a maze and wasn't an easy task. The church occupied two city blocks and had seven banks of elevators and a four-hundred-foot tower. I soon learned that the church had everything in it but a swimming pool, (almost like a YMCA). There was a gym, a bowling alley, a theater, a radio station, a parking garage beneath the church, numerous chapels, class rooms and dining rooms, as well as two assembly halls and much more. In those years, I recall the information, passed along in staff gatherings, that from nine o'clock Sunday mornings, when the church opens, to nine o'clock the following Saturday night, six to eight thousand people would have entered the doors of Riverside Church.

I was one of seven clergy. In addition to me, one was Hispanic pastor. All others were White. And I discovered there were seventy-five full time staff persons needed to run such an establishment, plus numerous part time and paid program leaders. The saving factor for me was my youth ministry and the teens I was called to serve who were not too unlike the ones left behind in Minot, except for ethnicity, race and class. There were over three hundred Junior and Senior High School kids who represented the proverbial rainbow of God's humanity and typical of New York City. They were Asian, Hispanic/Puerto Rican, White and Black and from all walks of life, coming from many types of public schools to private and prep schools. They came from the extremes of public housing to wealthy and privileged homes and apartments. Engaging them into the Christian Education facet of the church's ministry was the challenge. Enabling them to bond by being exposed to each other in their studies and the extraordinary programs we offered was the goal.

The successes outlived the failures and, with the aid of extraordinarily fine lay leaders from the congregation, plus students from Union Theological Seminary across the street, we, as they say, built the plane as if it was already in the air!

It was the Christian Education Department of Riverside that really embodied the best image and focus of the church's claim be Interdenominational, Interracial, and International. These were both challenging and rewarding times with an abundance of resources to carry out the programs we initiated. Also, at a time in the 1960's when the civil rights movement was at its peak and more adults of color (some the parents of our young people) were attending worship and joining the church, Dr. Martin Luther King, Jr. preached on several occasions. Most of the issues confronting our society and young people were integrated into our youth program as we did our best to confront the issues surrounding them, along with liberal Biblical studies as we understood them at the time.

My life was somewhat bifurcated between the somewhat stodgy all-White staff I related and reported to and my heartfelt, energetic, curious, fun-loving teenagers with all their other needs and problems.

By the grace of God and the extraordinary support, love and help from many, I settled into this new world, committed to giving it my best over the next six years. I brought a different and new perspective to Riverside, its staff and members which was appreciated and well accepted, though it was not ALWAYS what they wanted to hear or accept – GLORIA IN EXCELSIS DEO!

I love the quote by Teddy Roosevelt who said that had it not been for his years in North Dakota, he would never have become president of the United States. This giant step for me reflected Roosevelt's sentiment, echoed in my call to Riverside Church from North Dakota. Riverside Church found in me, a Black man who was comfortable working there with both White and multiracial teens and adults, because of my five-year experience in ND. I was a perfect fit for the job they needed with the multiracial and multi-cultural teens coming to RC.

It's been 60 years since leaving North Dakota, but my connections there remain powerful. When word reached me, through her granddaughter Debbie Harris, that Edna Keiser had died, Debbie did not have to ask me about my promise. I mentioned to her that I would make every effort to attend the service, thinking to myself, "Thank God it is in April and not the winter months!"

All the plans came together, and I left Philadelphia, flew to Minneapolis, and took a small plane from Minneapolis to Minot. The weather was not balmy but was clear and somewhat cold. However, it was a North Dakota spring-type day. Twenty minutes out of Minot, a snow squall came out of nowhere, jerked the plane around —"Fasten your seat belts" — and more.

The pilot, now on his descent into Minot, tried three times to land, but finally gave up and announced he was unable to land in Minot and he would take us to Bismarck. But, as North Dakota weather and God would have it, just as the pilot completed his message, a ray of sun appeared and opened an opportunity for the pilot to make his landing in Minot. "God is good!"

I believe it was Edna, both thanking me for coming but also, reminding me of ND weather so I wouldn't forget my years there – weather and all - and the joys we shared in Berthold.

I was met by Debbie Harris, Edna's granddaughter. She and her partner, Kevin Overland, were hosting me during my stay for the funeral in their lovely home. All went well after that.

Snow lay on the ground, and yet it was warm enough to turn to North Dakota mud. Debbie and Kevin had invited the old Y group for a potluck wine and cheese gathering in their lovely home. Fourteen gathered. Unfortunately, although Vivian Maragos Zimmerman was instrumental in calling the old friends together for the occasion, her husband, Dudley, had become ill and she was unable to attend. Per usual, we had a fabulous time; sharing old stories, becoming reacquainted with their families, and what their grandchildren, plus former Y and community leaders, were all about.

Before we all departed, and several guests had to travel to Bismarck, I put out the question (the same long burning one in my mind), regarding my presence among them and if I had made an impact during my time there? I hesitated and, unfortunately, decided not to use the word "race" in asking the question. Their answers were most affirming with anecdotes, laughs, serious reflections and more. But, once again, I had failed to get the desired response.

The funeral for Edna was in the Lutheran Church in Berthold, of course. That is where she and Fred moved their membership when the congregational church was dissolved. Arriving in Berthold gave me chills and an emotional high. It was only the second time that I had been there since leaving in 1957. That little town had become somewhat of a suburban bedroom community for folk working in Minot, including at the Air Force Base. There was now RUNNING WATER, paved streets, and a spiffy and attractive Main Street.

The new Lutheran Church (it was new to me), was beautiful, and with the parsonage, consumed the block that, during my day, housed both my church and parsonage, as well as the Lutheran parsonage and church. I was amazed and deeply impressed.

The service was moving and lovely and the church was packed. My homily went as planned and was well received (I made sure of that after the Minot disaster). The pastor was very hospitable and welcoming, especially since he had to forego the honor of delivering the homily.

Even before the service began, many Berthold families, friends and the like swarmed me to fill up my memory as to who they were and how much they appreciated my time with them. The ladies looked beautiful, many with tinted hair, lovely dresses and make-up and, yes, their pretty hand-made aprons, like the ones I recalled from my first community gathering the evening I first arrived in the fall of 1955. So, although it was Edna's home going, I felt like it was my homecoming. I never hugged and kissed so many Berthold ladies in my life!

Part IV

"When any white man in the world says, 'Give me liberty or give me death,' the entire world applauds. When a black man says exactly the same thing – word for word – he is judged a criminal and treated like one, and everything possible is done to make an example of the bad (n---) so there won't be any more like him."

- James Baldwin *(The 1619 Project)*

"Unremitting poverty, massive income disparity, cultural alienation, and human environmental abuse, to name a few. Christian social justice is in a world in which cooperation, community, compassion and charity of Christ are prominent and to which all other things are subservient for the common good."

- Ideas of Richard Rohr

"If you are in neutral in situations of injustice, you have chosen the side of the oppressor."

- Archbishop Desmond Tutu (1931-2021)

"Race remains a potent, divisive source in our society."

- Former President of the USA, Barack Obama

And What About Race?

I am basically an optimist, and I had to be in the issues of race and social justice work. I have devoted my entire life to this noble endeavor.

But I have to say that these are toxic times in which we now live. The social, racial, class and ideological divides among us are among the worst we have seen in our history. I say this even having lived through the Great Depression and civil rights struggle. This is deplorable!

As I head toward my own personal finish line, approaching my centennial, I believe my observations of the times I have lived through and the times in which we live now have some special currency.

As a result, I am aware of the importance of looking forward while learning from the past. In this memoir, I have found it strengthening and insightful to look back to my North Dakota years. Memory can gather light from the past and, hopefully, shed it on the present and the future. Therefore, I would be remiss if I did not return to the parallel themes that have guided me in life and in this book – race/social justice and pastoring.

The most complex of all is how race played out in my sojourn in North Dakota. I am sure current race theorists, social scientists, sociologists, and prognosticators will scrutinize this more thoroughly through the lens of their discipline and understanding, rather than taking at face value my existential experience.

However, I am compelled to pay attention of the most critical issue of race and its excessive negative effects in our country in the past that have gone onward into the present. The so-called justice system continues to work against Black people. It continues to be dangerous to walk peacefully or drive or jog while Black. This cannot be condoned!

I have yet to discover how I ended up in all, unexpectedly, or predominantly White communities, housing, and social gatherings from a teenager seventy years or so to the present time.

The "burning question" that sashays throughout these pages, as I try to both read the prominence of the issue of race in the assumptions, body language and subtle and unmindful discriminatory statements of my White constituents, especially young people, has revealed no closure in a way that fits into my experience and frame of mind.

Did I make any difference? That is the question that continues to haunt me. In other words, did my quest back then and even today have a positive racial impact? Regarding North Dakota, "Did my presence, my Black body and personality impact or influence the lives and social thinking of my YMCA teens, staff and associates or Berthold parishioners, and friends?" Furthermore, "Did the fact that I was Black ever translate meaningfully into my young people where, if ever they had to take a stand on racism or make a difference, did it happen?" Better yet, "As they moved out of Minot into the far-flung reaches of America and beyond, got married and into child-rearing, at any time did they draw upon their experience of knowing me, their Black youth program director?"

I am hoping that the experience – close at range or beyond in their lives – create in them an insight to be critical racial thinkers and, as a result, enabling them to stand up for what was right, just, and equal on behalf of Black people or people of color or, as we say today, "the other?"

To put it bluntly, did they move from complacency into action?

Returning to my tenure in Berthold, as said before, I asked my closest friends, the Keiser's, about how the discussion played out when I was under consideration to be their new pastor? They gave a resounding answer that it was never an issue. I still find that hard to believe.

Even back in the early 1990's, when I was in Arizona for business, near where Edna Keiser and her second husband were living for the Winter, I asked her that same puzzling question one evening at dinner. Once again, Edna's answer was the same.

How could that possibly be, I continue to wonder.

Race, in my Minot years, was not a big issue. In fact, the area was close to being devoid of racial animus, despite the stories I have mentioned about fathers demanding that their students withdraw from the Y due to my hire as their YMCA youth director. Recall that some of those same fathers hung out with Black women on Third Street. Or the time when I wasn't served at a coffee shop, while accompanied by some of my most loyal youth leaders. And two stepped up and took on the proprietor and told him that, if he didn't serve me, they would tear his place apart. And he immediately served me. These instances and other racial skirmishes, bordered on being major racist occurrences.

Given the history of race and racism in America and, looking back over six decades, what insight can I put forth for what appeared to be wholesale acceptance? My conclusion, not profound, but clear, sheds a different light on the issue there back in those days.

First, a few Blacks, as "tokens", have most always been accepted in major White societies. But if they appear arrogant or aggressive in pushing the "race" card, that acceptance is often short termed by the predominant White culture. Secondly, I often felt that when students, advisors, or others seldom, if ever, spoke about race, racism or about my Black lineage, that perhaps they were simply incurious when the issue of race surfaced. I believe they felt, even if they were to think about it, that race simply did not matter because they themselves weren't living it. They missed the point that the person experiencing racism certainly did know that it mattered. Finally, the geography and the sparseness of the population meant there were few occasions to encounter or be exposed to a Black person.

When the nation moved into the 1960's and the civil rights era of marches, non-violent demonstrations, and the burgeoning of new and more radical Black power groups, all working for the same principle of having Black people become first class citizens, that's when racism writ large became so detestable. We witnessed the destructive power of Jim Crow laws, lynching, police brutality and killings of Black people, vicious dogs. And of White housewives and mothers spitting on and hassling Black children trying to enter public schools and colleges. And so much more. This was the template for riots and disorder as people took to the streets seeking freedom, equality, justice, and inclusion in a multiracial and multicultural society.

It was at this point that President Johnson issued an executive order to establish the Kerner Commission for an in-depth study of race and racism in America. The commission's words of conclusions were short and succinct. They demonstrated that White racial discrimination was the root cause of unrest in America: "Our country is moving toward two societies, one Black and one White, separate and unequal."

So here we are, sixty some years down the road. Despite some progress, where do we find ourselves? As I assess it, not much has changed! In fact, I believe more White people now seem free to express their racist bias. What are those, appalled by this, to do?

To put it candidly, I have been engaged in a lifelong endeavor, testing my endurance, with a goal of creating racial understanding and respect. But this can't be a solitary effort.

As I have looked back at my North Dakota days, I continue to wonder whether my presence there was an anomaly, or did it really make a difference? Did those I mentored pass on the example of racial inclusion to their children and grandchildren?

To state it once again, did I make any difference? The more things change, the more they remain the same.

Indeed, some things have changed a lot since the Kerner Commission of so many years ago. But we're still a society deeply divided — Black and White. I can admit that some few things have improved for those who are Black. Nevertheless, the basic conditions really haven't changed. The power structure is still White, based on a superiority complex. And, as the demographics continue to change in this country, many of those who are White are getting anxious about how to hold on to their status. It's frankly all about keeping people in subjection.

There's a reason why those who are Black, when getting into leadership positions, are still seen as unusual and remarkable. I long for the day when that would be normal—not surprising or even celebrated and appreciated. We won't have true racial equality until we reach the point where what I have just described is the status quo. Otherwise, it is still seen as an uncommon achievement for Blacks to progress to positions of authority. The subliminal message is that equality is a gift granted through the largess of the White power structure—a grudging donation rather than a just allotment.

To be clear, people's heads and hearts are what need to change.

That is what I have been about all my life. Thus, there's my focus on whether there was a benefit from my interactions in North Dakota. As I mentioned earlier, did those I encountered, most particularly the teens that I mentored, as they've moved across the country, been enabled to have their eyes opened wider to racial disparities and, thereby, felt urged, spiritually, and emotionally and conscientiously, to make a difference with those they meet? That's the core of my anxiety. And I surely don't know the answer now. But you, having read this memoir, may be caused to think about this. If so, then I take comfort in that.

My lifelong experience has led me, in these ending days, to shine a light on my life in Philadelphia where my retirement community, Cathedral Village, is located.

Race still matters in this town, for sure, in the general population and even in my complex. My observation continues to be validated that Black people are more knowledgeable and sensitive about White people than vice versa. I remain someone looking for equality, equity, inclusion, and a greater degree of acceptance.

Two decades of my waning years have been spent in this wonderful continuing care retirement community here in Philadelphia. Taking stock of my life and years of being embedded and working within White communities on all levels, I have tucked away many of my findings, discernments, and understandings when it comes to race and living as a Black person with and among Whites.

One best example in my situation is to point out that ninety-nine percent of my fellow residents are Caucasians. When I became a resident, there were about nine other African Americans here. Over the years that number has waxed and waned, mostly the latter. There have been months and years in which I have been the only Black person in the independent sector.

This is a marginally liberal/progressive community of very fine people. Several times a year, I can count on some one or two persons asking directly of me or saying it within an earshot of my hearing: "Why can't we get more Blacks to come to Cathedral Village?" After all these years, I am laser sharp in discerning the privileged assumptions of White people. I could write another book about that.

I turn the question back on them by asking, "If Cathedral Village were a fifty-year-old retirement community, organized, built, and staffed by all Blacks — with the exceptions of a few token Whites, here and there, and the constituency raised the question: "Why can't we find more White people to make this their retirement home?" I move on to ask my White cohorts, "How many of you here would seriously consider or even come to a Black Cathedral Village?"

I don't ask for a show of hands so as not to embarrass anyone. I just leave that notion hanging. There's a great difference between a genuine versus a disingenuous response.

In a second chat with our Cathedral Village executive, which led to a focus on race, he ended the conversation by saying, "If we had as many African-Americans here as we have Jewish residents, the WASPs would all leave."

To my knowledge, one of the continuing bastions of all-White populations of privilege are found in retirement communities. Furthermore, with all due respect, not a lot of African Americans see it as a privilege to spend their final years with and among mostly White people.

So how much has changed over these years? Not much. The perspective of the Kerner Commission remains unchanged. Our society remains separate and unequal. Racism continues to distort, deny, and inaccurately report America's history. *The 1619 Project*, that honestly describes the enslaved arrival of Africans to these shores, is being staunchly portrayed by racists as voluntary! How absurd! Racists have been encouraged to flaunt their discriminatory attitudes and practices. All efforts are being made to deny there is discrimination. People of color are being prevented from voting for officials, who would truthfully represent them, by reconfiguring voting districts to shut them out. Those people of color most in need of a helping hand are systematically pushed further and further down the economic and financial ladder. Certainly, this is not fair, honest, or moral. And those who speak out against such injustices are labeled troublemakers and often are put in peril, sometimes through lethal means, to quell any dissent.

This is antithetical to what we say our democracy is all about. Are all of us created equal? Yes, indeed we are. But do those enforcers of discrimination believe this? Of course not!

We are awash in Christian Nationalism. Yes, Christians are the problem—certain kinds of Christian, I am ashamed to say. It's the right-wing White men who are provoking such mayhem in American society. They are entranced by political power over simple human decency. Their disdain for anyone who looks or thinks differently than them is irreligious and sinful. They are doing the Devil's work!

So, we have White people attacking and killing unarmed people of a different color, or faith tradition or country of origin (George Floyd, Breonna Taylor, Philando Castile, Ahmaud Arbury, and on and on and on), chants of "Jews will not replace us," and attacks on mosques. These same White men want to end abortion, primarily harming predominantly women of color.

Believe me, Jesus would be ashamed of these godless fear mongers.

What are the overwhelming societal problems that divide us today? Gun violence. Affordable health care. Attention to climate change. Insensitivity to the needs and concerns of others. Anti-immigrant bias. Cynicism.

There seems to be little concern for WE the people. Now it's ME the people as a commitment to selfishness.

We are living in a toxic, divisive, and dark time.

Here are three immediate ideas for positive change, that have enlightened me and a host of others, to move us forward or whenever we reach the other side from where we currently find ourselves.

1. Set up a Truth and Reconciliation Commission like the one that worked so well in South Africa. Spearhead it out of the Office of the Vice President. The goal would be to make it doable to listen, speak and learn.

2. Create a national Reparations Commission that acknowledges the problem and devises a way to implement it that is fair.

3. Create a National Youth Corp., requiring every young person at the end of high school or upon reaching the age of 17 to give one to two years of service to the country. The focus would be on efforts that enrich the societal good and build an urgent sense of commitment to service in creating understanding and respect across cross-cultural and racial lines, emulating the Peace Corp or Work Camp concept.

The basic commitment would be to invest in a mindset for the common good.

This is hard work, and it demands our attention. We all must join in creating momentum for such ventures. We know the reality of our crisis in America. Either we do something to make things better or we stay silent and just surrender.

I believe now is the moment to make a difference in these toxic and divisive times. Are you hoping that someone else will do it in your place? If not you, who?

This is a call to action. Each of us, in our own way, are called to join in this crucial effort! Perhaps, after reading this memoir, readers will develop a genuine commitment to creating a change in societal values. We must be inclusive, respectful, and committed people to make any significant changes.

In that conviction, I conclude this memoir with the specific challenge to join in this life-affirming quest.

Part V

"Teach us, good Lord, to serve Thee as Thou deserves; to give and not to count the cost; to fight and not to heed the wounds; to toil and not to ask for rest; to labour and not to ask for any reward, save that of knowing that we do Thy will…"

-St. Ignatius of Loyola

Better Angels

In his first inaugural address, President Abraham Lincoln
grappled with his uncertain and divisive times by calling for
guidance and support from the better angels of our nature.
His approach resonates with me since I also have been
blessed by better angels in my seasons of distress and grief,
and throughout my life. Therefore, I want to acknowledge
these divine messengers who enabled my successful journey
during the years when I lived in North Dakota.

Frances Dever

FRANCES DEAVER was an older teen when I arrived in Berthold. Avid church attender. She held positions such as Church School teacher, Vacation Bible School teacher, available to help under most circumstances and simply devoted to the church and firm belief in the Lord Jesus Christ.

Though I did not have the privilege of officiating at her marriage in the Berthold church, Pops Sharkey was on hand to perform her marriage to the love of her life, also a member of the Berthold Congregational church.

With all of that faith and commitment, life can often take one in a different direction, when least expected. Read the book of Job and other Biblical stories as examples.

Frances was resilient and managed to meet head on any adversity that came her way, not without grave detriment to her body, mind and soul. But through the years she never gave up. Jesus often said to people he healed, "your faith has made you well." And so, it has been with Frances as she has never given up.

By some set of strange circumstances, Frances took unto herself the task of being a news clipper and archive keeper of much if not all that Bob Polk did in Berthold, Minot and beyond. She often sent clippings from the Berthold Tribune about something I had done, my new work at the Minot YMCA and my penultimate call to New York City to be one of the ministers at Riverside Church. Worship programs or speeches in which I was involved, NY Times articles I may have sent to her, she returned as well as issues or projects in which I was involved in the state, worthy of an article in the Minot Daily News.

Through the years, I have enjoyed all of Frances' endeavors and have managed to squirrel most away with other Polk papers to go to the Amistad Research Center at Tulane University in New Orleans, LA.

My one quibble with Frances and the commendable, tidy work she has performed on my behalf over the years is that she often forgets to date items. Alas, I'm never sure of the source and date.

But all she has shared in epistles concerning her life, divorce, family and work, without losing her sense of personal identity with God and his faithfulness, along with her dainty, meticulous clippings dating sixty years ago and beyond, she ranks high on my list as a Better Angel in the many ways she has handled her life in the midst of crises and never wavered when it came to her faithfulness and her strong support of yours truly throughout these years.

Austin "Jim" Engel, Jr.

WHEN REV. ED TREAT and the Homeland Division of the Congregational Churches sought to strengthen its work among the Ft. Berthold Indian Reservation, they could not have selected a better person than Jim Engel. For over four decades, the mission on the reservation, faith based, cultivated, and nurtured by a strong social justice advocacy ministry was carried out by Rev. Harold and Eva Case. The Cases were a godsend to Ft. Berthold, known and loved by all the residents who was a strong advocate helping them to meet most, if not all, of their critical needs and problems – and they were legion.

Rev. Jim Engel, freshly graduated from Yale Divinity School, along with his wife Mary and their four young sons, picked up the gauntlet to be left when the Cases' retired. In his early years he worked close to Rev. Case and became aware of the social, personal, political, spiritual, and humane issues faced by the Ft. Berthold Native Americans.

Jim Engel and family moved to New Town in 1954 to help establish that community and church which had been relocated by the Army Corps of Engineers, hoping to mollify those Native Americans who moved there from their centuries old Elbowoods and all that transition entailed – mostly disastrous. Pastor Jim built the church membership, continued to provide spiritual, social, and political care for the new racially mixed population. He also served the neighboring church in Parshall, ND, continuing to be pastor to both Native Americans and Caucasians.

His work was so effective, and he was so well regarded, and his work, social action and empathy so greatly appreciated that the denomination moved him to work at another new church development in Bismarck. In 1965 he was appointed by the governor as Director of Indian Affairs for the entire state.

Jim was a lifelong Democrat, where in he 1972 became Executive Secretary of the NPL Party. Again, recognized for his outstanding accomplishments, the governor appointed him as Director of State Planning for the Native Americans.

Following this busy life of social responsibility and action on behalf of the Ft. Berthold community, he retired, attended law school, took his degree and practiced law in Bismarck and New Salem, ND.

Known for his ethical integrity, love of politics and hard work along with his passionate work for social justice; he co-founded with Eva Case, the Charlies L. Hall Youth and Family Services in Bismarck.

During my years as youth minister at Riverside Church, I established a work camp program. Fifteen students, multiracial, and so forth, with three advisors. I checked in with Jim Engel to see if I could bring a group of New Yorkers to Ft. Berthold for a five-week project. Jim agreed, found several Ft. Berthold teens to match ours. The two groups bonded superbly, worked diligently, and built, from scratch, a small community center for the Native American teens. Jim Engel was the kingpin, found all the contractors and was the "go to" person whom all of my youngsters loved and deeply respected for his life and work there. He spoke (lectured) several time providing the historical context of Ft. Berthold an how the US Govt. broke yet another of its treaties with the Affiliated Tribes at Ft. Berthold when it, the government, went in to build the Garrison Dam along the muddy Missouri River.

Without Jim, it could not have happened so smoothly, and he was on site each day to determine our needs and became part of our family group. Many wonderful moments – Kumbaya in the good sense. Some of my former young people still talk about it and one has revisited Ft. Berthold and has written extensively about our work camp effort and his experience there.

Mr. & Mrs. Fred & Edna Keiser

FRED AND EDNA KEISER, along with their two teenage children, were the first Berthold Church parishioners I met when taking that assignment of becoming their pastor. It was the Keiser's who came to Minot to Rev. Sharkey's house to meet me and fetch me out to Berthold, introduce me around, both at the church and within the community amid some implicit misgiving about me, a Negro pastor, being there.

From the old tested and approved sociological standard, the Keiser family was an outstanding couple, one of the largest farmers in the area. If Fred and Edna approved "it", it had to be okay. And so, it was with my coming, the first Negro to the Congregational Church and only Negro in the tiny town of 400 souls in Berthold.

My presence surely did not get blanket approval but with the Keiser's approval it had enough for a clean start. Fred was chairman of the Board of Trustees at the church and Edna busied herself in the Lady's Society and teaching both Sunday School and Bible School in the summers. Daughter Kay was a gifted pianist and shared playing for Sunday services along with another very fine pianist, Verna DeBilt. Freddy Keiser, Jr. was an active junior high school student.

It was the Keiser family who took me under their wings immediately. I spent more time and consumed more meals at the Keiser home than at any other, during my two- year tenure in Berthold.

For the uninitiated, back in those days and times in rural America, there was no private phone system. You had to crank the dial of the phone on your wall which in turn would alert the central operator in town and tell her where you wanted to call then she would do the rest. Which meant she not only plugged you into the number you called, but would listen in on your conversations. It was well known and straight up, for the most part, but with the Fred and Edna Keiser, early on, we determined that we had to have a coded system when speaking on the phone so dear Anna Dockin, our central operator, did not know all that we talked about. For example, once I shared with Fred and Edna that I could not manage taking a bath in a large, galvanized tub with one kettle of hot water, they jumped to my rescue and mapped out a plan. "Call and see if we'll be home" and ask, "is the Y available?" That became the green light for me to go to their home, have dinner with them, shower and watch Lawrence Welk most Saturday nights. The coded system worked and I clued my Chicago family in on the system so I did not spell out in detail how I felt and how I was getting along.

Fred and Edna also had a wonderful sense of humor. We could share stories and laughs in general. Issues related to the church and how I was doing were also in their purview. Their candor, discernment about my work with individual town's people and/or parishioners, meant I could always count on them for the right response and/or if I was naïve when it came to some people.

The Keiser's were my spiritual family away from home. There was very little we did not or could not share with each other and benefit from whatever the situation or issue.

Those town folk who were either not in favor of my presence or had questions were also some of the folks who looked for signs, especially how my parishioners dealt with some of the critical social and personal issues. For example, I often went with Fred and Edna to visit Fred's father in the Lutheran retirement home and got to know him modestly well. Prayers by me at the end of visits were in order. So, when he died, some folk in the town wondered if Fred would want me to officiate at his father's funeral or whether he would call Rev. Sharkey from Minot to take charge. Fred asked me. The town's naysayers showed up for the service and were pleasantly surprised at how I handled it.

As to race, I reached the point when I felt free to ask Fred and Edna if my race was an impediment for the congregation and town. The town was not all on board, but as for the church, they said, more than once, it was never an issue. I believed them and it was never explicit, despite underground rumors and some members, the husbands, who refused to attend worship or get involved due to my presence. Note, however, they were not involved prior to my coming. When trying to keep their youngsters from participating in the church of their baptism, some kids and mothers came anyway.

I am sure Fred and Edna had to put up with some of this talk in town, due to their support and closeness with me, but it never spilled over into our relationship or with their children. They were, in biblical terms, steadfast, never wavered, and faithful to the end.

Following my tenure there, we kept in touch. I had left the state when Fred died and could not attend his funeral but pledged that I would move mountains to be at Edna's service, should she predecease me. And she did and I had the great privilege of returning to Berthold to deliver the eulogy for dear Edna who, in over the sixty years since I left, we never missed each other's birthday and being in touch throughout the years.

Gloria in Excellus Deo

Everett E. Miller

BORN AND REARED IN and around the Twin Cities, Ev Miller was an authentic Minnesotan. He was a physical education major graduate from the University of Minnesota. People, YMCA, sports and administration were his main interests and life's work.

Miller's tenure as General Secretary followed Minot's founder—the person who worked in every quarter of the community to bring the YMCA into Minot, and who died suddenly of a heart attack, Colin Brown. The Minot Y Board and the public were so close to Brown and his magnificent addition to the community, it felt no one could ever fill his shoes. It did not take long for Ev Miller to carve out his own leadership and direction for the Y and enable it to move forward, building upon Brown's philosophy, but taking it to greater heights and in a new direction.

Ev and his wife, Dorothy, had two preteen children when they moved to Minot and soon were a part of key aspects of Minot's social, educational, and daily routine.

Miller was a fine administrator who continued building and improving upon the staff Brown left. I like to think of him as a "teaching boss" who found purpose, strategy, and encouragement in whatever it was he motivated staff members to do. He was never arrogant or insistent, but always believed and pointed out a better way.

Ev was a people person, easily engaging whomever he was talking to, either an individual or a group. He was even given to sharing much of his own background as he related numerous stories and anecdotes to drive home his message.

He was an all-around person who could fit well into any situation and find meaning and purpose: a great athlete, outdoorsman and fisherman who was competitive and still humble in his one hundred percent commitment to the history, philosophy, and work of the Young Men's Christian Association. He made sure his senior staff was deeply indoctrinated in all things YMCA and afforded them (us) the opportunity to take courses, attend workshops and meetings related to Y history and… its purpose.

He gave his all to the Minot Y, its Board of Directors, the Y's Men's Club, its major service organization, community, and religious leaders. An all-around, gregarious person and the consummate face of the Y in the City of Minot.

Miller was a devoted member of the local United Methodist Church, Rotary Club, other religious and civic clubs in the city. He was well respected by all segments of the city with whom he came into contact. He was also very interested in the lives of children, young people and their families. The Y was a family and co-ed program place for all and not just young men, with membership rolls to prove it.

No doubt when Ev pulled off his coup and brought me on staff as his Youth Program Secretary, I am sure he took a lot of flak and criticism from several of the more racist naysayers who never let him forget their disdain for Negroes, especially in a leadership position and directing their children and youth.

As an outdoorsman, he often took a group of businessmen on camping, canoeing and fishing trips in Northern Canada and to the pristine wilderness country in Minnesota. These were trips his laymen cherished forever.

Rev. Forrest B. "Pops" Sharkey

"POPS" SHARKEY was like the gadabout pastor in Minot before and during my tenure at Berthold. Or, like a celebrity, he managed to be a part of or show up at most of the critical and important events in Minot.

Feisty, somewhat portly, his eyes were always on the prize and, regardless of your church, faith, or denomination, if he was needed or any injustice was committed, Pops was always on hand, especially for the underdog or the disinherited.

First Congregational Church of Minot, though not one of significant membership, compared to the larger Lutheran Church, and with a smaller building, it still ranked among the important churches in the city. Pops helped to make it such and wore its importance and emblem on his chest. Known throughout the city and relevant to most issues, especially those related to the social gospel, he was never shy in expressing his opinion of some of the critical issues facing the city and its environs.

A great raconteur, song leader, youth advocate and social activist, Pops was the go-to-pastor for not only tea and sympathy, but for updated, critical liberal thinking and theology. He was not appreciated by many but that was who he was.

He was probably the Y Board member to get Ev Miller's attention about bringing me to Minot and keeping a focus focusing on championing the Youth Program at the Y. He served as one of the bridge builders when it came to racial justice as it found its way into the wider community.

His heart, head, mind, and spirit all worked together when it came to social justice and the importance of one or more people making a difference in any given social responsibility.

I was always a welcomed person in his home and with his family, like so many others who became a part of the Sharkey's' family had extended to both church members and beyond. His wife, Marcell, had her own prominent role in a community at the Y where she was the office manager.

My last conversation with Pops was after he had been notified of the passing of his son George. How fortunate I had been to be the only person from his life and family to be on hand at the close of George's life. Pops seemed grateful for that coincidence. And how blessed I was to be able to be like family to pray with George, hug him and represent his home and family on that sad occasion. Pops died soon after George's passing.

Rev. Edward Treat

"...But love and I had the wit to win, We drew a circle
that took him in." - Edwin Markham Adapted

OF ALL THE YEARS OF MY traversing for our church's national youth work and more, and at a time when the national church was decrying racial prejudice, discrimination and injustice, it was simply demeaning, disingenuous and sad during my seminary career to have State Conference Ministers (bishops in some denominations) visiting with me, back slapping and delivering words of encouragement, but never attempting to find a church assignment, either as a summer student intern or to candidate for a full time post. All Congregational churches were independent and did not take orders from Conference Ministers.

The one most likely to step up with the encouragement of seminary classmates who had worked in North Dakota, was Ed Treat who managed to visit with me and explain the dearth of Negroes in his state and say he honestly had no idea how any of his churches would react or feel having to decide on hiring a Negro, either as a summer intern or a fulltime pastor.

Candid and deeply spiritual, social activism was not visible in his speech or in reaching back to his days growing up or in college or seminary. He simply did not expose his feelings, attitudes or assumptions concerning Whites and Blacks comingling. And certainly, that was not an issue in the state of North Dakota.

He seemed to have got religion somewhere, perhaps pulled it up from his childhood or the denomination's new policies concerning how churches and members should pave the way for national tolerance and trust, and come together, in the spirit of Jesus Christ.

In the spring of 1953, following our meeting and my assurance if he located a church interested in bringing me on as its summer intern minister, I would accept, follow through and take the job. All of this happened, and I was appointed to work with the pastor of the Congregational Church of Garrison, North Dakota.

The social, racial and personal trauma as spelled out above was more than Rev. Treat had bargained for. It almost tore that church apart and Treat had to spend more time healing, reconciling, and pampering that church than he had bargained for.

He held to his social action and deep faith position in directing the church and working with individuals within the church, to the extent that he realized he had come to grips with his sense of social and religious responsibility in doing the right thing. That even lifted his personal being. And he knew he was standing for the right values and principles of the church and for the denomination's initiatives in one of the least expected places in the country – North Dakota.

Tall, gaunt, with great depth and a slight resemblance to Abe Lincoln, this was a deeply spiritual devoted husband, father and pastor, He weathered the storm he never dreamed he had a part in committing.

The same was true when I needed a church following my ordination and no option in sight. Ed Treat called and offered to help, once again, and he did! This time around, he was familiar with the race battle and had prepped himself on Blacks in North Dakota and how that Nordic population reacted to racial tolerance and understanding.

In my two-year trial assignment at the Berthold, ND Congregational Church, Ed was front and center, both to the people of that congregation before and up to when I took up residence. He put himself on the line, took the flak from his Board of Directors and others, felt he was on solid personal and theological grounds from his perspective and took superb care of his "token" Negro pastor. He had my back and I always felt it in his presence or from a distance as others passed the word on.

Vivian Maragos-Zimmerman

VIVIAN MARAGOS, a beautiful, smart, critical thinker, compassionate and talented, found her niche by becoming a volunteer at the Minot YMCA and the advisor to the senior class of high school girls in Tri-Y after graduating from high school. She was the daughter of first-generation immigrants from Greece. She was the only daughter of nine children and was strongly committed to her family, the Greek Orthodox Church and her Tri-Y girls at the YMCA.

The cultural standards of her parents prevented her from attending college. She would have been a stellar student by anyone's standards. But this personal difficulty was turned into an opportunity for her to benefit others by becoming the advisor and star volunteer to the Y as one who led by example.

Vivian invested her curiosity and quick mind as a volunteer to the Y for over eight years. She shepherded the most popular girls club and participants were devastated if they could not get in. It was not like a sorority, but it was THE club. And Vivian, with all of her charm and grace, nurtured her young ladies in a way no one else had or could. She was a trusted adviser to successive classes of senior high young ladies. Vivian was a motivator and the students in her club captured her commitment. Each in the club bonded together in such a way that they pledged to remain closely related following their high school days and be dedicated to service and the Y.

For over six decades, when any of her former students are in town or visiting, they always seek her out to connect with her. She would usually host such groups in her home. This is indicative of her influence and the connection they maintained over the years.

Vivian was marvelously astute and self-educated, meaning that she could measure up to any college degree student getting high grades. She was impressive because of her critical and reflective thinking skills, combined with her quick wit, compassionate nature, and counseling expertise. She was my "go to" advisor and we had a special collegial relationship. I listened to her and discussed challenges with her and always came out better for her insights and perspectives. She was also a great team player along with other staff and volunteer workers.

All her eight brothers had significant connections with the YMCA, either in membership, its Hi-Y programs or at other levels and respected its work and influence in the broader community.

Following my departure as Youth Program Secretary at the Y and given an interim period, filled by one of my former youth leaders, Bill Blore, the Y hired a full time Youth Director from Wisconsin, Dudley Zimmerman. Vivian continued her outstanding volunteer services to her Tri-Y young ladies, and, before too long, she and Dudley became a great team, fell in love, and were married.

Vivian and Dudley had five sons, all of whom have done well. The Maragos family, a strong force within the Minot community, ultimately followed in their parents' footsteps and became entrepreneurs and established a leading hospitality and hotel business in the city. Vivian, though behind the scenes at times, was a key player and motivator in this new family venture.

Unfortunately, Dudley died a few years ago. That was a devastating blow to Vivian and the family. However, it has been gratifying that she has managed her grief, picked up the gauntlet and returned to serving the needs of her family, church and community as in the days of yore. She has been an extraordinary memory checker for me as I have plowed through writing this book and at times, our phone chats are quite lengthy, remembering.

Vivian, as well as I, have remained in touch with a large swath of our former Y students. When they write and visit Vivian, she passes along greetings they send me and when I am in touch with others, they always ask about Vivian and send best wishes.

She has left a major footprint on Minot and, as I say in my Minot Y section, on most of my volunteer advisors, plus staff who have kept close to the Y philosophy. More importantly, we all have endeavored to lead by example, especially Vivian.

The town has changed so much and most of our former young people have moved away and return mostly for family and high school reunions. Vivian has never been properly honored for all she has contributed to her students, church, family and community. Thus, this Better Angel is special among the others and, if I had the power, given her years of selfless, meritorious service to the Y, her church and the wider community for all these years, she would richly deserve the LIFETIME ACHIEVEMENT AWARD! I would have the entire community gather to proclaim this honor to how she has demonstrated the positive paths to a wholesome life of love, dedication, and service.

If we all gathered in one room to develop a plaque honoring Vivian, the caption would read:

TO VIVIAN MARAGOS-ZIMMERMAN
in whom the inner and outer are one

Lois Polk Graham

SISTER LOIS WAS THE oldest of six siblings and considered the black sheep among parts of the family; she dropped out of school at the end of junior year. This was to the anger, dismay and horror of my parents, who, as Negroes, felt the only way to a better life was through education.

In many large families, like ours, it was not atypical for the oldest sister to take on responsibility for the youngest born child… which was me. She was the "big sister" who took responsibility (along with my mother) for nurturing me, until I became a teenager and quite independent of my parents, Sister, and all authority. At this time, we are talking about pre-WWII. Jobs were difficult to come by, even with a high school education, but especially if one was Black, female, and had not completed high school. Our mother found an ad in the daily paper of a White family in the South Shore; a wealthy, White community, looking for a maid. The salary was seven dollars per day, five days a week, and on-call as needed for special occasions involving entertainment on weekends. You know the drill...washing, ironing, shopping, cleaning the house, cooking, and of all things including helping "the Madam" care for her several Shetland sheep dogs she helped breed. All of this for seven dollars a day!

Though diminished by family in those early years, Lois was strong, humble, faithful, and resilient, holding up her place in the family, either in spite of or because of her station in life. She was well liked by her cadre of friends who seemed not to be bothered by her new status as a maid and high school drop-out.

She retained her fondness for me and vice versa through the years. She was always making sure I did not make the same mistake of dropping out of school and always conscious of the company I kept growing up; making sure they were of good caliber.

On the other hand, due to her demeaning job and comparing notes to family and neighbors who were also domestics, plus the racist environment surrounding us, she was not shy in expressing her dislike for White people. She was a bit miffed when I started fraternizing with more White people than Black and let it be known via reminding me of the way White people treated Negroes. When White friends came to visit in our home, and if it was an overnight visit, she was the one who gave up her bed for them to sleep. Often, she said that "I'm tired of giving up my bed for Bobby's White friends."

When WWII began, she became employed in the war factory with a number of her friends and her wages were increased considerably, along with her self-esteem.

She taught me so much about life on the "other side" – the White side, that is. And though she loathed White people and my taking up with them, she always made sure I was well prepared for meetings with them (meaning look presentable, have enough pocket change for eating out, tip well and always send thank you notes when I visited and stayed overnight with others).

As I began to get into the topic of church and race relations, I realized it was not just the Whites I was working with that needed help in multi-racial understanding and tolerance, but within my own home, family, and friends. It was hard work on both fronts.

Lois (who, by the way, was the sister that gave me the title of this book), was the only sibling who remained at home. Even when she married late in life, she brought her husband to live in the homestead. She was the caregiver to both parents until the end of their lives. She was truly one of the saints to give this much love and devotion.

Sister Lois taught me, among other things, how to be humble and grateful, generous, and kind to other people (whatever their station in life) and especially those underappreciated, underdogs or lowest persons on the totem pole. Her wit, insight, generosity, and compassion for others impacted my life and has served me well over the years. Unlike the rest of the family, she was not a church going person, but deeply spiritual and she lived a life of service of me and others to the glory of God. From her I will always remember to never be bitter or cynical. For this narrative, she tops the list for my Better Angels.

Solo Deo Gloria!

The Ties That Bind

I have spoken about those who have made a significant impact on my life, but have not provided a fuller profile of me as an individual and professional worker for justice and a more inclusive/welcoming society. Therefore, let me spell out my journey up to this very moment. Here is a brief background on what has helped me and shaped my interactions with others.

After leaving Minot, I spent six years as the Youth Minister at The Riverside Church in NYC, after which I served for two years as the Dean of Chapel and Dean of Students at Dillard University, one of our Historic Black Colleges in New Orleans, LA. I then returned to NYC and went back to Riverside Church as its Minister of Urban Affairs and Outreach.

My personal life enlarged on 1968 when I married Flora Ford, a former church school teacher and a youth advisor at Riverside. In 1969 we adopted a seven-year-old biracial son and made our home in Manhattan in a three-bedroom apartment on Fifth Avenue overlooking Central Park. It was our custom to always offer hospitality to both old and new friends. Over the years, in the midst of so many endeavors, my marriage ended in divorce, and I have remained single. Unfortunately, our son, George died in 1999.

My efforts to provide for and create a better society have included serving as the Executive Director of the Edwin Gould Services for Children and Families, providing foster care and adoption services. I later became the Executive Director of the New York City Council of Churches where I spent ten years — as well as in several other interim positions.

Over the years I have been graced by many honors, including a doctorate from my alma mater, Doane University, in Crete, Nebraska. I was the first

Black male student and the first African American to earn a degree there. In recent years I inaugurated an annual lecture series there on race and social justice to promote public and candid conversations about current social justice issues and race across the country and the world.

Following my (official) retirement, I served as an interim pastor in several Connecticut churches and as Vice President of Community Affairs at City College (CUNY). Throughout my career, I have served on numerous boards and committees, including The Alvin Ailey American Dance Theater. For the past twenty years, I have made my home at Cathedral Village, a continuing care retirement community in Philadelphia, PA, where I have produced an annual Black Arts Festival, held annual services in honor of Martin Luther King, Jr., inaugurated a successful three day mini Bach Festival, established a Barbershop Quartet and kept active in many of the other program offerings here.

I turned ninety-four in May 2022

NOW BACK TO CITING notable individuals and emotions that made a special mark on my life.

For example, when I open my "guest book," which I have kept for over fifty years, there are many names that stick out for me, accompanied by fond remembrances. Stroll down memory lane with me.

- **Five Minot businessmen** and community leaders came to visit upon their return from a cruise to England and back. Their desire was to see how I was doing and to have a first-hand look at Riverside Church, often referred to as the Baptist cathedral, built by John D. Rockefeller, Jr.

- **Three Minot students,** now in the military and about to be deployed overseas, disembarking from NYC, took an extra day before leaving to visit, be shown around, catch up with me and catch me up on Minot, break bread and share the fruit of the vine.

- **Vivian Maragos (Zimmerman)**, and **Robert Jagd, Jr.** —These deserve the highest tribute. They were adult advisors who gave meritorious service, commitment to their students and set high standards in leading by example in the principles of the YMCA. Mr. Jagd was a Junior High School teacher and advisor to the Jr. Hi-Y club of

twenty-two members that made that exciting and somewhat daunting trip to New York City in 1960.

• **Jim Paul,** who attempted to expand his Minot haber-
dashery skills in the New York market for a brief time before returning to Minot.

• **Diane Barsness,** Steve and the Barsness family gathered with me for lunch at International House, located
near Riverside Church and Columbia University.

• **Wes Hiller** – on a solo driving trip to NY and Eastern
USA, located me. Wes Hiller is a famed high school basketball champion and hero who set many records. He also
was a Hi-Y club member. He made a three-day visit to
NYC and my home on Lake Candlewood in Connecticut.

• **Andy Fedders and Leon Miller,** standout Minot
High scholars who were admitted to Harvard University,
spent their first break with me in NYC during the city's
crippling snowstorm. They arrived before the city was
shut down and they managed to scoop up enough snacks
and beer to last until traffic started moving again. On a
trip to Harlem, they had an encounter with a White
rookie cop on the beat who pulled them aside with racist
overtones. We were in view of Riverside Church at a distance, to which they pointed, and told the cop I was a
minister there and their godfather. He scurried away
without looking back.

• **Bill and Mai Robinson** – were former Minot high
teachers. Bill was the drama coach and Mai Nagatomo
Robinson taught English. They elevated their positions by
becoming professors at Grand Junction College in Col-
orado. They invited me to be a guest speaker at the col-

lege and they visited NYC every year with students, taking in massive amounts of Broadway theater. I always met on one afternoon or evening with the Robinsons and their group. Later, Mai's unexpected illness and death led Bill to contact me to conduct her memorial and burial in a Chicago cemetery set aside for Japanese Americans, where all of the Nagatomo family was interred.

• **A Minot student** (I won't reveal his name) arrived in NYC and contacted me. Months later he called and invited me to officiate at his marriage, which was to be in his girlfriend's apartment in Greenwich Village. Dinner was to fol-low. My wife and I arrived on time, but it took an hour for the couple to come into the living room where the service was to take place. At issue, among other things, there was a heavy aroma of weed — so much so, I could hardly get through the service, and I doubt if they understood anything I said. I have had no word from them since.

• **Everett & Dorothy Miller,** I kept in touch with my former boss and good friend, Ev Miller, over the years. That was primarily via Christmas cards and letters that his wife, Dorothy, had a hand in. My leaving the Y on such a short notice and checking that out in hindsight, it is wonderful that Ev even wanted to stay in touch. Nor did I bid him farewell properly. Everything happened so quickly. All of this occurred before I was tutored to send thank you notes on significant occasions, especially one like leaving a job on a positive note. But notes and a few spare phone calls from Ev were welcomed and he would give me the rundown on Minot, the Y and friends. Ev resigned from the Minot Y some years following my departure. He became executive director of a large YMCA in the town of Everett, Washington. As luck would have it, many years later, I had the good fortune to go on an assignment to

Seattle, Washington. And, of course, I immediately
thought of Ev and Dorothy Miller and saw that Everett,
WA was close enough to Seattle for a visit. Ev was chair at
a Rotary Club meeting on the day and time I was to arrive.
Dorothy drove to Seattle, met me, and drove me back to
Everett. We were to go right to the meeting which Ev was
chairing. And we did.When it came time for new business,
Ev took the privilege of introducing me. He was a bit emotional and chocked up in the process and I almost followed
suit. However, he was quite gracious in his words about
me and our work in Minot.

Following the meeting, we went to the Millers' lovely home and spent
the afternoon catching up. They drove me back to Seattle where we had dinner
and concluded what was a magnificent day of reunion and renewal with
friends who were like family to me – back in the day. He created a moment
that I cherish and deeply remember.

• **Susan Davy,** She is one of the top potters in North
Dakota and the country and always attends the Annual International Craft Show in Philadelphia. It was my custom
to take in the show, on the evening of the last day, when
Susan would pack up and we would go to dinner and
spend hours talking about Minot and other mutual concerns. A few years ago, when I wanted to share a genuine
ND Wild Game Dinner with friends here at Cathedral Village, my retirement community, and not knowing if I
could pull this off, I reached out to Susie for help. I requested the possibility of pheasants. A few days later I received five or six pan-ready, iced down pheasants with two
recipes along with a roll of venison sausage. I added the
other parts of the menu, wild rice, salad, cranberry sauce
and more. My seven guests will never forget that sumptu-
ous evening and the goodies from ND.

- **Don Anderson,** Don was director of the fitness center, which included being the aquatic instructor. He was a graduate of Minot State Teachers College and was a great colleague at the Y. Many of the Minot population, children, and adults, learned to swim thanks to Don. The young girls all swooned over him, not only for his impressive looks, but for his way with people as a coach, instructor, and role model.

Ev Miller encouraged Don to attend George Williams College, a YMCA college in Chicago, hoping he would consider become a professional certified YMCA staff member. When his parents moved South, Don became keeper of the family home. Off to Chicago, he asked me to rent and care for the house while he was away. I obliged and enjoyed overseeing a lovely Minot home. George Williams College was not exactly a good fit and Don returned to Minot where we became housemates for the next several months before my departure to New York. I enjoyed good times with my fellow staffer who always enjoyed a party.

Don had also left behind the love of his life, Joyce, also a student at Minot Teacher's College, which hastened his return. They were married and I recall the gala celebration with all who gathered in Joyce's hometown. Whenever I return to Minot and the old Y group gathers, it's a happy event when Don and Joyce are among them.

- **Armend Lynner,** He was our business manager at the Y, now called the CFO, and he was always on duty, kept the books, reported to the Board of Directors, and never missed a beat when it came to keeping the Y in the black. He was industrious, committed, thorough, and efficient. His head was always down in overseeing and working the numbers. Armend was a great staffer and part of the young Turks, though less talkative than the Minot State interns and other staffers, Armand was front and center as part of our cohesive and productive staff. I shall always recall the time when Armend and his fiancé, Re Nae, asked me to officiate at their wedding the day before Thanksgiving. I did it and they have been married for close to sixty-five years now! Again, whenever the call goes out for a reunion with Bob Polk, Armend and Re Nae know there will be a party and always join in.

• **A Letter Came** from one of the Tri-Hi-Y young ladies who was homesick, starting her first year of college and unsure about what to expect. She reported that the first Sunday, following Vespers, there was an all-campus sing-in. They sang, among other songs, The Ash Grove, which I had taught them at one of our YMCA Sunday gatherings. How much better she felt, she said! There was never another note, and I assumed she did well.

• **Joel Davy, Jr.** He had Thanksgiving dinner with me and my wife, son and others the year he was in NYC for a special study assignment. He never forgets sending Christmas cards. This year's P.S. reads: "From one of your Hi-Y kids with fond memories of that wonderful trip to NYC, thanks! (No mention of the communion cups – ha!)

• **Bill Blore** visited NYC and spent time with me and my family, had dinner and took in a Broadway musical.

• **Kenneth Leigh,** On a business trip to the West Point military academy, he came to visit me and my family in NYC before returning to ND.

• **Senior Hi-Y student** leadership "Lifetime Award "— This would go to Bill Blore and Kenneth Leigh, who taught me everything I knew about being a youth director (their words!). Inadvertently, they became my eyes and ears and were sensitive to my special needs and those of their peers. Known as "scrappers," that label came in handy more than once. They were team players, had innate leadership qualities with high standards and they always had my back. Bill Blore succeeded me as interim Youth Director at the Y following my resignation.

• **Two Black couples,** They were dispatched to the Radar Site south of town. Their stay was short, but once we connected, it was a joy to be united with my soul brothers and sisters. One was a great jazz and blues singer who performed at one of the Main Street cafes on weekends. Whenever the occasion presented itself, we gathered, let our hair down and insulated ourselves from the world around us. We simply felt and enjoyed our roots and shared personal stories of the moment.

• **George Sharkey,** Pop's son, visited during a business trip to NYC and we had dinner at the Russian Tea Room, which impressed him no end. There he told me of his brain cancer. A year or two later, I was in Billings, MT where George lived. I discovered he was hospitalized. Upon a return visit, George was in Hospice care and what appeared to be an end-of-life situation. A young couple from his church and I were his only visitors. During some agonizing moments, we stayed the course and offered many prayers with George. Before boarding my plane early, the following morning, I had a call from the hospital informing me of George's death. I immediately phoned Pops. He had already been notified and thanked me profusely for being with George at the close of his life.

• **Mike Wold,** This is an amazing story! Mike was in my Y-Boys choir and about ten years old when I last saw him. He seemed to have remembered me and when his business sent him to Philadelphia, he located me, and we agreed to have dinner on one of his free evenings. I was to meet him in his hotel lobby. Devil that I am, I said to him, "Mike, when I walk in the lobby, you'll recognize me, but I don't think I will remember you." We laughed and had a glorious dinner and evening catching up on the many years between then and now. Mike later attended my 90th birthday party at Riverside Church in NYC and months later, he and his wife, Rosann, came to visit Philadelphia, sheltered in our Guest House, and spent quality time visiting and catching up, in the evenings, following their days of being tourists.

• **Pam Costain,** She made contact to come and visit and spent time on, among other things, race, and social justice issues. She billeted at the Cathedral Village Guest House, and we engaged in ample dialogues and discussions. One of her interests, related to my years in ND as a Black person and how did I manage and feel? Or, in more bold terms, what was it like? Truly, this is the burning issue of my life. Pam's parents were among my Minot friends. Prior to her visit, she was about ten years old when I last saw her. Pam was strongly involved in social responsibility, and so forth, in Minneapolis. In 2020, when George Floyd's excruciating murder took place, and all that followed, including Black Lives Matter, Pam was a rich resource for me to call and have first-hand information.

• **Phil Costain,** Following our group Jr. Hi-Y visit to West Point, where he so graciously hosted the boys, Phil remained in touch. In his senior year at the Academy, he requested I be the officiant at his wedding at West Point Chapel. This was an honor indeed!

• **David Waldron,** He was a long-standing friend dating back to my Berthold parish days. We explored issues of current interest, trips down memory lane and took time for significant dialogue. He was never out of touch. This was especially true when Carson Wentz was quarterback for the Philadelphia Eagles. I received several phone calls per game when they were doing well (smile).

• **John Kildahl,** My Connecticut lake home and retreat was near Danbury, CT. John read an article by or about me in the Danbury paper and made contact. Visits with him and his wife happened often. I discovered that John had become a fine baritone soloist and, on a couple of occasions, was the special soloist at the church where I was interim pastor.

• **Debbie Harris and partner Kevin Overland,** Debbie is the granddaughter of my dearest Berthold friends, Fred and Edna Keiser. Debbie and Kevin generously and graciously hosted me at the time of Mrs. Edna Keiser's death and fu-neral. I spent quality time visiting all of Edna and Fred's family during that period of grief and sadness. It was Edna's "homegoing" and my homecoming in Berthold, at the Lutheran Church which she and Fred joined after the Congregational Church was sold and removed. The new, stately and beautiful Lutheran Church and parsonage took up the entire block. I delivered the eulogy for Edna. Dur-ing the repast it was my opportunity to meet and greet ol' timers of Berthold. What a joy it was to be remembered and to hug and kiss so many old timers. Debbie and Kevin also hosted a magnificent evening gathering of former Y staff and friends. Debbie and Vivian set it up earlier but unfort-unately, Vivian's husband Dudley took ill and they were unable to attend. Again, it proved to be a great evening of catching up and comparing stories as we traced our paths down memory lane. I tried, once again, before the close of the evening, to raise my burning question, "How did my person and presence affect their lives and those of our Y youngsters?" I could always count on Bill Blore to lead off. His tenor and tone were reflective and somewhat ego satisfying. And others chimed in saying how much they appreciated me as a person and my leadership. What I was hoping for, and what never surfaced, was how my presence as a Black man had any consequence then or now?

• **Marly Balsokat Bergerud,** She always sent an annual Christmas greeting and letter, updating her life, her business, her favorite son, her writing, and most recent social life.

• **Carol Carlson,** Carol was a youth member of the Garrison church where I served as summer student minister. Her career as a teacher was in US military installations around the world. She settled down and married and moved to NYC. We were in touch often. But she died far too early and I officiated at her funeral at the request of her husband. Her sister from Garrison attended the service and, if my memory serves me well, the sister was the nurse that called upon me to baptize the breached baby that hot, scorching August morning in Garrison.

• **Dixie Walker,** Cards, emails, letters over the years had come from her home in California and she is never out of touch. We made contact when she was in New York, where she shadowed me around when I made a couple of pastoral visits. It gave her an idea of how some folk lived in the Big Apple. The one dowager's home we visited was one of the most unique places to live in Manhattan, Sniffen Court. Dixie and our host got along well in that our host had never met anyone from North Dakota. Dixie was a great trooper!

• **The Hon. Robert Wefald,** I saved this for the end as
a personal heart-warming story you all will enjoy. Bob
spent a great deal of his time on Amtrack between New
York and Washington, DC. Often, his mid-way stops would
be to Philadelphia to visit me for a lunch, drink and, as
always, a recounting during these amazing visits as to all
that kept Bob engaged. He was truly the lifeline between
ND and me. It was always quality time to catch up with
him in his terribly busy, high profile, national and
politically related schedule. On one occasion, his wonderful and industrious wife, Susan, accompanied him. Their
home is in Bismarck.

Bob always had so many balls flying in the air, I could
not keep up with them all. But I do recall him introducing
the idea of chairing a campaign to raise funds to have a US
Submarine named after the state of North Dakota. This
was just one of the ventures he reported on in our visits.
During one visit, Bob reminded me he had achieved his
submarine project and brought me up to date with the
events that followed. All of which amounted to the events
leading up to the commissioning of the submarine and, as
chairman, Bob was involved in giving oversight to portions
of that project, such as the dinner the night before the official commissioning with a large ND delegation, fund con-
tributors and more. It was for that occasion that Bob
requested that I offer the invocation for the Chairman's
Dinner the night before the final and official launching.
I was simply blown away and it didn't take too much
nudging for me to say yes. Bob considered me as a former
son of ND and how appropriate he felt that would be.
This was to be a special kind of prayer I had never delivered. One of my fellow residents here at Cathedral Village,
Dick Anderson, was a former submarine officer. I spent
time talking with him and reading material he passed

Bob standing in front of the USS North Dakota

along. In crafting my prayer, I also called upon a former colleague, Roy Lloyd, communications specialist at the National Council of Churches and a great word maven. He edited my draft, and we came up with a proper and fitting invocation for the occasion. I was seated at the table with the commander of the USSND and he assured me that the prayer would be visible for his crew and paid high complements. I will remain grateful to Bob for this daunting but memorable assignment.

• **"Having the blues"** is a term used in the Black community denoting despair, aloneness, feeling jumpy, downhearted, forlorn, temporarily unhinged, and loveless! These are feelings that come and go and are often stated by our elders, who might say, when asked how they feel, say "I got the blues today." Everyone understood that. When I would have the blues and reached the point of despair or melancholy, with no one like me around to share or converse with, especially with a personal issue or racial resentment, there was simply no personal social intercourse. So, I got the blues. I often fell back on my ancestors, parental struggle, neighbor buddies and so forth, I would take time to reminisce about days of bygone times, personal faith, lines from scripture or favorite hymns, blues and jazz ditties, Black poets like Paul Laurence Dunbar and many others. The one true paragraph that captivated my thoughts were the words by W.E.B. Du Bois statement from *The Soul of Black Folk:*

"It is a peculiar sensation, this double-consciousness, this sense of always looking at oneself through the eyes of others…One ever feels his twoness, — an American, a Negro; two souls, two thoughts, two unreconciled strivings; two warring ideals in one dark body, whose dogged strength alone keeps it from being torn asunder."

• **Census update,** Sixty years after my ND days, the state has become one of the most diverse states in America due to numerous factors: military installations, federal government employees in Bismarck, higher education, the oil industry and more. However, from all indications, the issue concerning race seems never to have been a major problem, even with an increasing percentage of African Americans in the state. As I have mentioned several times, when I became a registered citizen of ND, I was informed that I was the forty-eighth Negro in the state in 1955. Though I have made that statement often, with current research, I doubt the validity of that. However, not seeing another Black person for months and more, I felt like the only Black human being in the state. When I applied in person for my driver's license, the clerk looked right at me and checked my race as "White"! I kept that ND driver's license for years showing my Black friends and telling them

I was "passing."

> Census update – 2020:
> ND population – 760K
> African Americans – 21K
> Minot – 40K
> Berthold – 500

This is just a sample of the three hundred plus young men and women we served at the Minot YMCA during those years. Many have distinguished themselves both in their careers, home, family, and community lives. And each year I learn of those whose lives have ended, some sooner than others. We would be remiss not to salute them. It is precious never to forget those who have gone before. We will always have them in our hearts and prayers as we joyfully recall our lives together.

In many of our in-person chit chats, Vivian and I muse about those years and times and recognize the vast changes in our society for six decades. We always conclude that what we experienced then would not be possible even a few years later, but especially today with young people.

My conclusion, these years later, and in all of my multicultural endeavors and jobs, is that racism and its many manifestations of prejudice, discrimination, segregation and inequity, is like the conclusion of the old Rogers and Hammerstein song: "You've got to be taught to hate and fear, you've got to be taught from year to year, it's got to be drummed into your dear little ear, you've got to be carefully taught…"

I shall have to keep reformatting that question about racism to, hopefully, learn more deeply about how race played out there. I am inclined to think it simply made no difference, back in the day, or even in today's toxic racial environment back in ND.

In this era, time, location, social climate and lack of either exposure to or education concerning the beautiful and diverse world in which we live, we must always continue in the struggle to overcome these divisions.

I do need to express my heartfelt love and appreciation for those dear former Y students, co-workers/colleagues and friends who have kept the eternal flame of friendship burning. Those I have had direct contact with — friends like Vivian Maragos Zimmerman, Bill Blore, Ken Leigh and others mentioned above — were wonderful helpers as we reflected on and gave substance to what we collectively were able to do, back in the day.

We have often tried to give words that had the special kind of meaning we felt existed between our young people. There was an esprit de corps, a tight knit community of Y teens and, better yet, my old word from youth groups was fellowship. Vivian offers the Greek word, Koinonia which gives an even fuller depth and energy to our work then — and now.

Whenever my dear mother, returning home from a trip or attending an upscale event in Chicago, her first words in affirming the event or trip were: I wouldn't take nothing for my journey." In closing this, my journey in the Great State of North Dakota, I would echo my mother's words followed by a resounding Amen!

My Soulful Antecedents

This old Norwegian saying speaks volumes, especially for me: "Too soon I grow old; too late I grow smart." Another glad surprise was the day I received in the mail a book about African Americans in North Dakota. It came three decades after my sojourn there. This book: AFRICAN AMERICANS in North Dakota, Sources and Assessments clearly reveals what I never knew about the state and its Negro inhabitants. As a matter of fact, I was either incurious or simply assumed that Black people had little or no history in the northernmost state of the Great Plains. And it wasn't until I read the book that I was exposed to the reality that Negroes were indeed part of the historic tapestry enveloped in this massive land becoming a state in 1898.

I was told that I was the forty-eighth Negro in the entire state upon my arrival in Berthold in 1955 (recent research proved this to be in error), and that was an historic feat, as many would say. No doubt I was caught up in the traditional American history teaching which seldom brought to light the rich culture and history of African Americans, Native Americans and more before, during and post-civil war. In retrospect, I should have known we were here along with, and in some cases, before the White settlers.

The book and other sources point out that the earliest Negroes, we are told, came as slaves to the first explorers and traders. Others were a part of opening of the territory along with the Whites before it became a state. I was intrigued with the book, its title and content. In scanning it, I also found my name, associated with my two jobs, Berthold, and Minot.

Along with the explorers Lewis and Clark was York, a Black man who accompanied them through the Rocky Mountains to the Pacific and back. We also learned that in those early days, African Americans were homesteaders; worked on the steamboats, were cattlemen, railroad workers, homesteaders and in harvest crews. They were also baseball players and regular working men and women. Some who came out after the Civil War, included the 10th Cavalry in 1893, buffalo soldiers, called that by the Native Americans who said their hair reminded them of the curly buffalo hair. And, yes, there were Black cowboys. In all my childhood and youth growing up and movie going, I had never seen a Black Cowboy. Blacks also came to homestead and start a new life like their White counterparts. Clusters of Black communities were dotted across the vast landscape.

The book goes on to say that Blacks came and went in every moment of North Dakota history: the "wood-hawks" who cut timber along the Missouri, the roustabouts on the steamers, the cowboys, the women servants in the homes of the early day gentry and the soldiers posted to the Black regiments on the frontier.

The authors of the book often spoke of racial assessments as being somewhat of a mixed bag as Negro communities sprung up in towns and rural areas across the state. One lynching was reported, but also many racial incursions, mostly inconsequential, except noted for the moment in the local papers.

Four portraits that give insight into how some Blacks made it and were achievers in the Peace Garden State.

York was already mentioned above who served with Lewis and Clark.

The great and indomitable Satchel Page, the legendary baseball pitcher of all times who played with the Bismarck interracial baseball team.

Era Bell Thompson, reared in ND with her family, a graduate from Morningside College in Iowa, she ascended as a distinguished writer/editor for Ebony Magazine, the African American iconic Johnson Publication. Her outstanding book, American Daughter, was called to my attention by Bob Wefald, who gave it a stunning review in the Bismarck Tribune.

Riley Rogers. I was caught off guard when I came across this name. Rogers is a Chicago boy, and we grew up in the same neighborhood, West Woodlawn. Roger's father was a medical doctor in the community. Rogers found his way to Jamestown College in North Dakota, graduated from the

University of ND and took his degree in pharmacy. Married and with family, he lived the rest of his life in Valley City, ND. At one point, he was elected Mayor of the city.

All I can say, in thinking of these soulful antecedents, is that they blazed a trail, and I followed their path.

Prayer for Submarine

USS NORTH DAKOTA
COMMISSIONING SERVICE
CHAIRMAN'S DINNER
24 OCTOBER 2014
GROTON, CT
INVOCATION DELIVERED BY THE REV. ROBERT L. POLK

LET US PRAY:

Our God, Our Help in ages past,
Our hope for years to come,
Our shelter from the stormy blast,
And our eternal home.

0 DIVINE SPIRIT, CREATOR OF HEAVEN AND EARTH, SUN & STARS, WIND, WAVES AND SEA; WE COME BEFORE YOU ON THIS GLORIOUS COMMISSIONING OCCASION TO BLESS THIS REMARKABLE VESSEL; THE ENDEAVOR OF GREAT MINDS AND HUMAN HANDS.

MAY ALL WHO SERVE ON HER BE PROTECTED FROM THE PERILS OF THE DEEP AS THEY GUARD OUR COUNTRY. MAY A SAFE COURSE ALWAYS BE PLOTTED FOR HER SONS AND DAUGHTERS WHO LIVE AND WORK ON BOARD AS THEY TRAVEL THE WATERS OF THE WORLD WITH VIGILENCE AND COURAGE AND PERSONAL RESILIANACE.

0 GOD, WE PRAY THAT EVERY VOYAGE IS FILLED WITH THE GIFT OF LEARNING, ENCHANCED BY COPING WITH CHALLENGES THAT DEVELOP SKILL, CONFIDENCE AND EXPERTISE.

MAY SHE ALWAYS BE A TRUSTWORTHY AND RELIABLE PARTNER WITH YOU TO BE GUIDED THROUGH STORMS AS WELL AS WATERS OF CALM TO A SAFE HAVEN AND A FRIENDLY PORT.

WE PRAY THAT THE USS NORTH DAKOTA WILL BE LOYAL TO THIS GREAT STATE BY BEING MINDFUL OF ITS GLORIOUS CREST WHICH EMBRACES THE SYMBOLS AND BEARS THE WORDS: "STRENGTH FROM THE SOIL & REAPERS OF THE DEEP."

WE IMPLORE YOU, GRACIOUS GOD, TO MAKE THE STORMY SEAS OF LIFE TRANQUIL BY YOUR HEAVENLY BENEDICTION. AS STATED IN THE BOOK OF PSALMS, WE KNOW YOU CAN STILL THE STORM TO A WHISPER AND HUSH THE SEAS. SO WE ASK THAT THOSE WHO SAIL ON THIS BOAT ARE GLAD WHEN IT GROWS CALM AND ARE SUCESSFUL IN THEIR MISSIONS.

FINALLY, MAY THOSE WHO BECOME ONE WITH THIS GREAT VESSEL LIVE OUT THE ENCOURAGING THOUGHTS OF MARK TWAIN BY THROWING OFF THE LINES, SAILING AWAY FROM SAFE HARBOR, CATCHING THE WIND AND, IN DOING SO, EXPLORE, DREAM AND DISCOVER.

Invocation cont. -2-

WE COMMISSION THIS GREAT BOAT, USS N.D. AND ASK YOUR CONTINUED BLESSING ON ALL THE SOULS SHE WILL ENCOMPASS AND PROTECT.

We are grateful for this occasion -the Chairman's Dinner -and all who gather about these tables for nourishment, fellowship and the joy of your many blessings.

GOD BLESS THE USS NORTH DAKOTA, ITS NAMESAKE AND GOD BLESS AMERICA. AMEN.

BENEDICTION

Go forth into the world in peace;

Be of good courage;

Hold fast to that which is good;

Render to no person evil for evil;

Strengthen the faint hearted;

Support the weak;

Help the afflicted;

Honor all persons;

Love and serve the Lord;
And may the blessing of God almighty be with you, the USS North Dakota, its commander and crew now and always. Amen.

Rev. Robert L. Polk has lived for the past nineteen years in a retirement community in Philadelphia, along with four hundred other retirees. At times he has been the only African American resident. There he has authored two other books: *Crossing Barriers & Building Bridges, a memoir,* and *Tight Little Island*, a montage on his West Woodlawn community, located on Chicago's South Side. Polk is an ordained Congregational (UCC) minister and has held positions in North Dakota as pastor and YMCA youth director, New York City, at The Riverside Church, at Dillard University in New Orleans, LA as Dean of Chapel and Dean of Students, and other positions. In retirement, he has served interim pastorates in New Fairfield and Washington, Connecticut.

www.ingramcontent.com/pod-product-compliance
Lightning Source LLC
Chambersburg PA
CBHW050452110426
42744CB00013B/1967